Marriage: Work & Warfare

A Self-Help Manual

For Healthy Marriages

LORENDA GRACE ADEGBAYI

Copyright © 2014 by Lorenda Grace Adegbayi
All Rights Reserved

Published by Aim 2 Love, Inc.

Printed in the United States of America

ISBN 978-0-9839567-6-1

This book or parts thereof may not be reproduced in any form without express written permission of Lorenda Grace Adegbayi.

Unless otherwise noted, all Scripture quotations are taken from the King James Version of the Bible.

Scripture taken from The Message. Copyright 1993, 1994, 1995, 1996, 2000, 2001, 2002, Used by permission of NavPress Publishing Group

❧ DEDICATION ❧

To my husband, my priest, my strong man, my friend, my lover, my bed warmer, my luggage carrier, my chauffeur, the one who covers me and is covered by our God and more:

The man who loves his wife, Akinyemi Richard Adegbayi, who has helped me to walk out the truths in this book.

Thank you,

From your wife who respects and loves you.

❧ PREFACE ☙

Marriage: Work & Warfare was birth out of the lessons I learned as I embarked on my new life of marriage. I was prepared for the work. I am very disciplined and hard work has enabled me to achieve most of my goals. But the warfare was totally unexpected. Even more disturbing were the people the enemy used to launch his attacks on our union.

Many years later, after the work both my husband and I put into our marriage, we have been victorious in keeping our marriage strong in the midst of warfare. Today, as the wounds of the past battles are healed, we are enjoying our life together.

There are three areas that I focus on for couples to **Work** and **Wage War** to achieve and maintain a healthy marriage. They are **Communication**, **Intimacy** and **Oneness**. Many problems in marriage are limited to these areas. I begin with God's original intent for marriage. None of the problems existed in the Garden of Eden. There was no need for work or warfare until man sinned. The one act of disobedience changed mankind forever. It also, changed the marriage relationship forever. Strife between the husband and wife that began in the Garden is ever present, seeking to divide what God created to be indivisible.

Thanks to the shed blood of Jesus Christ and the victory He won over the enemy of our souls, we can enjoy marriage the way God intended. It is my prayer that everyone who reads this book will be armed with the informational tools that can be easily applied to have a healthy marriage.

❧ Table of Contents ❧

Introduction 1

Chapter 1 - The Beginning 5

Chapter 2 - The Work of Marriage 13

Chapter 3 - The Work of Communication 19

Chapter 4 - The Work of Intimacy 27

Chapter 5 - The Work of Oneness 37

Chapter 6 - The Warfare of Marriage 45

Chapter 7 - The Warfare of Communication 51

Chapter 8 - The Warfare of Intimacy 59

Chapter 9 - The Warfare of Oneness 69

Chapter 10 - The Characteristics of a Healthy Marriage 77

Chapter 11 - The Communication of a Healthy Marriage 83

Chapter 12 - The Intimacy of a Healthy Marriage 87

Chapter 13 - The Oneness of a Healthy Marriage 91

Chapter 14 - Conclusion 95

MARRIAGE: WORK AND WARFARE

INTRODUCTION

To understand marriage, I had to marry. Theories from the books I read and testimonies from people I knew only scratch the surface of preparation for the new life I entered on my wedding day. Some alluded to the work of marriage, but none prepared me to expect spiritual warfare; none taught me how to stand against the spiritual attacks, especially those from loved ones.

Although the warfare began at the announcement of our engagement, the work was yet to come. We overcame and prevailed against the odds through prayer, faith in God and the belief that our marriage was our God designed destiny. Notice that I did not mention love. We did and still do have love for each other, but love without faith, prayer and purpose would not be enough to weather the turmoil that was sent to destroy our union. The unconditional love and support from my husband that began on our first date has been strength for me and has kept me when everything and everyone seemed to be against us. Now God uses us to be light to others, helping them find purpose in their marriage.

This is the book I would like to have been available during our short courtship. It is a simple, practical manual that will help married couples rekindle intimacy, communicate more effectively and understand the significance of being one. Those who are unmarried will be enlightened regarding the struggles that so many couples face and learn how to safeguard against them. Those who have suffered the pain of divorce will better understand why their marriage failed and how to build future relationships on a firm foundation.

All failing marriages do not end in divorce. Those that do end in legal divorce are over 50%. Those that do not go through the courts, increase this number significantly. Some couples may not legally go to the courts for dissolving their marriage, but they are

Introduction

spiritually divorced with or without physical separation. That is, they are no longer one flesh. They can live in the same house, sleep in the same bed, but their hearts are far apart. They are no longer connected in their purpose for marriage.

Divorce, whether legal or spiritual, does not bring glory to God. This is not God's plan for any marriage, even yours. I believe the most common reason for divorce is not money or infidelity, but selfishness. Selfishness is when concern for one's self or own interests are considered above or more important than that of the well-being of others. Quarrels that spouses have over money or any other problems are rooted in one spouse not being willing to consider how their actions will affect the other. If both spouses are willing to reevaluate their marriage through a proper understanding of Scripture, the source of problems will be revealed. Your marriage can recover, but it takes two. One person cannot save a marriage. Both spouses must at some point be willing to do their part to restore the marriage.

This book will help strengthen healthy marriages for the long haul. It will be a healthy marriage road map for those who are experiencing difficulties. For those who are in the process of healing after divorce or loss through death, you will find reassurance of God's ultimate plan for marriage and prepare you for the next season of your life.

The Woman Every Man Should Love

She is attractive, but ignored by many.

She is desperate for attention, but few notice her.

Many pray to get her, but most cannot identify her when she appears.

There are many counterfeits, but there is none that comes close.

She is God sent, but not often received.

Who is she?

She is Wisdom and she waits for you to fall in love with her.

                Find her in the book of Proverbs.

        Poem by: Lorenda Grace Adegbayi

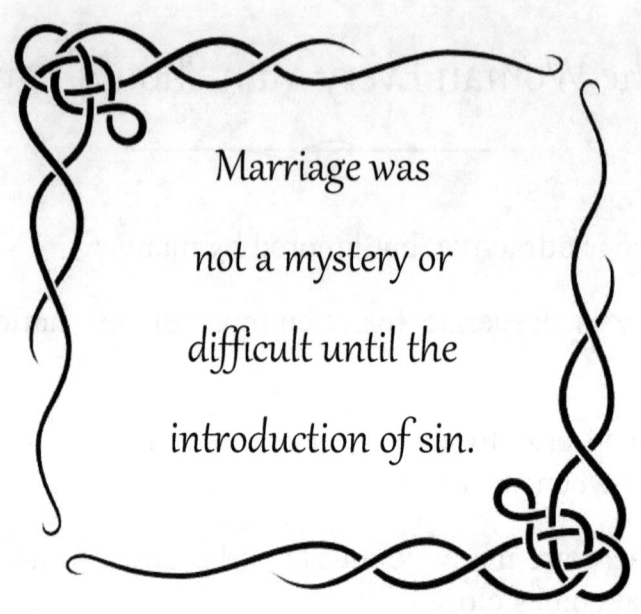

Marriage was not a mystery or difficult until the introduction of sin.

Chapter 1
The Beginning

Marriage is part of God's original design for mankind. Twice it was recognized by God that Adam needed a helpmeet. In Genesis 2:18 when He created Adam, God said, "It is not good for man to be alone. I will make him a help meet. " In Genesis 2:20, there was not found a help meet for him. It was not Adam who looked at the animals, which all had a mate, and then desired a mate. It was God's idea, not Adam's. Scripture never records that Adam desired a mate.

Everything God created was created good, including marriage. Marriage is defined as the social institution under which a man and woman establish their decision to live as husband and wife by legal commitments, religious ceremonies, etc. In the beginning, man and woman joined together and became one flesh. There was unity and agreement between them. They were naked and not ashamed. Each was comfortable in being and doing what they were created to be and do. It was not until the serpent began speaking words of doubt to the woman that they deviated from God's plan. Marriage was not a mystery or difficult until the introduction of sin.

Sin means to miss the mark. Sin is against God and separates man from God. In Genesis 2 when Adam sees woman he calls her "bone of my bone" and "flesh of my flesh." She shall be called woman, for she was taken out of man. She did not look like any of the animals he had previously named. Something about her was different. Adam was asleep when God removed his rib and formed woman, but instinctively he knew she was of him. Adam did not reject his mate from God, but fully accepted her. He did not question why he was to share his dominion with her for he knew that she was him in a different body. He embraced her into his world. God agreed with Adam that she was part of him and described this union as the

Chapter 1 – The Beginning

two becoming one flesh. This union of two becoming one is what today we call "marriage".

This union of one flesh was so strong and the order of God, man and woman so perfect, that Satan had to study it to see how he could get man to separate from God. The separation between man and God would ultimately lead to separation between man and woman and tarnish the original intent of marriage.

Satan had been in the presence of God when he was an archangel. Ezekiel 28:14-15 He knew the character of God, but did not know the totality of God. Satan knew that the command was given to man not to eat of the tree of the knowledge of good and evil. This command was given to Adam while the rib that was used to form woman was still inside of him. Man and woman were both God's administrators of earth. The command was given to Adam, but woman was to obey it, also.

Man was given only two commands in the Garden. The first command was permission of what he could eat. The second was the prohibition of what he was not to eat. It was the boundary that Adam was not to cross. This was the only limitation God placed on Adam. God commanded the man to freely eat of every tree of the garden, but of the tree of the knowledge of good and evil, he was not to eat of it. The day that man ate from the tree of the knowledge of good and evil, he surely would die.

Genesis 2:15-17 "And the Lord God took the man, and put him into the Garden of Eden to dress it and to keep it. 16 And the Lord God commanded the man, saying of every tree of the garden thou mayest freely eat: 17 But of the tree of the knowledge of good and evil, thou shalt not eat of it: for in the day that thou eatest thereof thou shalt surely die."

Because Adam and the woman had no knowledge of evil, only good, they were an unsuspecting target of Satan's plot. Satan knew he could not dethrone God. He had already tried to dethrone God and lost his heavenly position. Satan knew man had been given dominion over birds of the air, fish of the sea and every living thing that moved upon the earth. If Satan had any chance of disrupting God's plan, he would have to find a way to get to the man to disobey God.

The Bible describes the serpent as subtle or crafty among all the beast of the field. Subtle means difficult to detect, requires mental acuteness and cunning. Crafty means skillful in underhanded or evil schemes, cunning, deceitful and sly. Satan used the serpent because the serpent's character would be an easy cover for his plan.

The serpent was known to be subtle. So why did the woman participate in conversation with it? Her conversing with the serpent should have been from the position of exercising dominion over it and not subjecting herself to be questioned and manipulated by it, especially when the serpent misquoted God's instruction. The woman eventually succumbed to the temptation of the serpent. Adam should have corrected the woman and the serpent before the act of disobedience was committed. When Satan through the serpent began to talk to the woman and question God's word, Adam also did not exercise dominion. Why was talking to the serpent no big deal to Adam or the woman? Could they have had the ability to communicate with animals in the beginning?

When the serpent contradicted the woman's interpretation of God's command, why did the woman accept advice from the serpent instead of standing on the word and character of God? Both man and woman had been given dominion over the serpent, but did not exercise their dominion. Instead they subjected themselves to the

Chapter 1 – The Beginning

ungodly wisdom of the serpent, which led to their fall. When we do not enforce our dominion, we will lose our authority and become dominated by something or someone else that was never intended to dominate us.

In Genesis 3 we see the result of disobedience. Once Adam ate the fruit offered to him by the woman, the eyes of both of them were open. It was the beginning of man and woman sensing the need to hide from God. God is love.

> *I John 4:16 "We have come to know and to believe in the love God has for us. God is love, and whoever remains in love remains in God and God in him."*

They were both made in the image of God and had a close relationship with God. They were God's agents or managers on earth. Through one act of disobedience, this was lost.

This disobedient act led to the beginning of physical work or labor. The serpent no longer had legs to walk, but was sentenced to crawling on his belly. Now it forever slivers through life on the ground eating dust. The woman was sentenced to conception and child bearing in sorrow. The pain of childbirth is generally overcome by the joy of new life. On the contrary, the struggle that resulted from the fall between the wife and husband would be one that every marriage has to deal with. In the beginning both man and woman were different, but one did not have rule over the other. After the fall, the wife's desire would be to her husband, but God gave him the responsibility to rule over her.

The sentence for disobedience for Adam was physical labor. He would have to work the ground for food. God also gave a death sentence. Human bodies were designed to regenerate, restore and repair itself. As a result of the fall, this physical body would no longer live forever. Now the body whose nature it is to repair itself would have an antagonist working in it to oppose its creation purpose of regeneration. This internal opposition is the very nature of sin. Sin means to fall short of intended target or goal or purpose. This opposition to regeneration is what ultimately leads to physical death. Death will eventually return the body to the dust from which it was taken. This is the beginning of the work and warfare of marriage.

Chapter 1 – The Beginning

Marriage: Work and Warfare

Study Questions

Chapter Study Questions are a great way to allow what you're learning to work in your heart and mind. Please start a journal to enter your answers to chapter study questions. We recommend not writing your answers in your book, as answers can be very personal.

1) Who instituted the first marriage?

2) What was God's original intent for marriage?

3) God knew man needed help managing the earth. God's idea of help for man is a _____.

4) Harmony between God & man, man & woman was disrupted by _____.

5) What is the root cause of separation?

6) Define sin.

7) The fall of man resulted in the lost of relationship with God, loss of dominion, loss of the Garden of Eden and problems in _____.

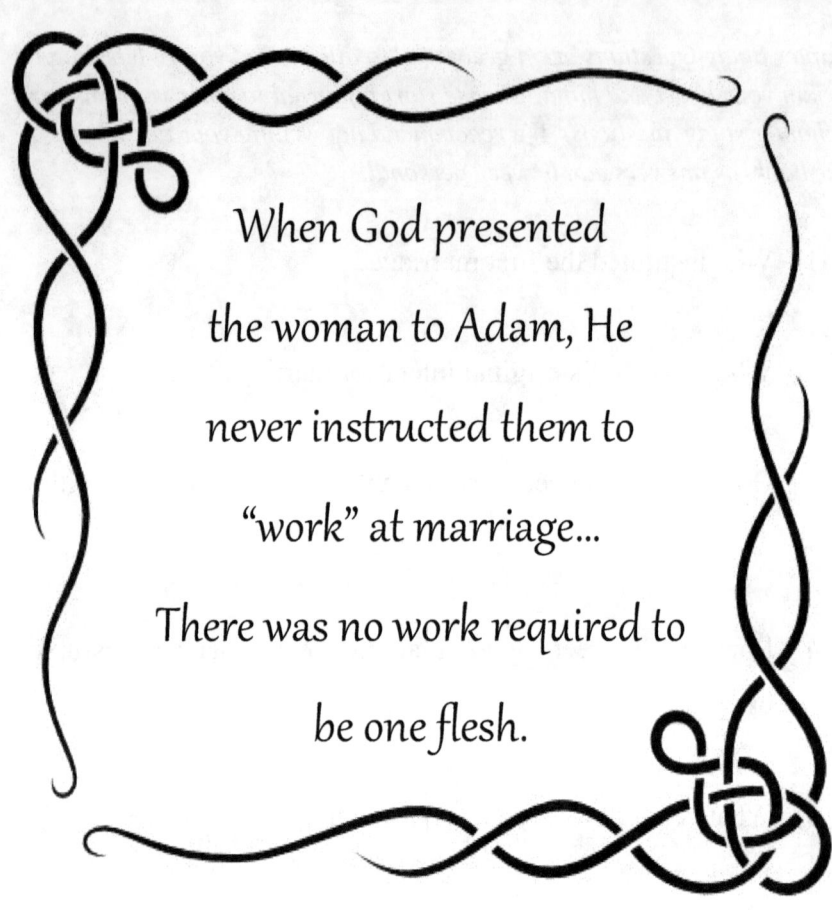

When God presented the woman to Adam, He never instructed them to "work" at marriage... There was no work required to be one flesh.

CHAPTER 2
THE WORK OF MARRIAGE

Work is defined as exertion or effort directed to produce or accomplish something; labor or toil. What we describe as work today is very different from what was considered work in Genesis chapters one and two. When God created the earth He did it by speaking what he wanted and it manifested. What he spoke into existence, He gave power to reproduce more of its kind. Therefore, once God created creation, it reproduced and God did not have to create the same creation again. Reproduction was innate and a natural part of the life cycle. Note that before Genesis chapter 3, the life cycle did not include death, only life. Everything God imagined and spoke came into being. Once it manifested he called it "good", because it was exactly what he intended it to be and did exactly what it was created to do.

In the beginning God created heaven and earth. When God creates something it is exactly what He intends for it to be. Therefore, the heaven and earth God created in the beginning was not created without form and void. An event took place between Genesis 1:1 and Genesis 1:2 that changed creation from what God intended, to it being without form, void and dark. The event that disrupted creation is described in Isaiah 14:12:

> *"How are thou fallen from heaven, O Lucifer, son of the morning! How art thou cut down to the ground, which didst weaken the nations."*

The order was disrupted when Lucifer rebelled against God. In Genesis 1:2 we see creation that is now without form, void and covered with darkness. The Spirit of God hovered over the earth awaiting God's instructions. When God spoke, His Spirit manifested

Chapter 2 – The Work of Marriage

what He spoke. The disrupted creation is being transformed into an ordered earth in Genesis 1:3-31. In Genesis 1:31 God concluded that everything He made was "very good".

John 6:63 confirms that it is the spirit that quickeneth; the flesh profiteth nothing and that the words that God speaks are spirit and are life. Before the worlds were framed by the Word of God, and things which are seen were made out of things which do not appear (Heb. 11:3), when the whole mass of inanimate matter lay in one undistinguished chaos, "without form and void," we are told that, "the Spirit of God moved upon the face of the waters" (Gen. 1:2). There are other passages, which ascribe the work of creation (in common with the Father and the Son), to His intermediate agency of the Holy Spirit. For example, we are told, "by His Spirit He hath garnished the heavens" (Job 26:13). Job was moved to confess, "The Spirit of God hath made me, and the breath of the Almighty hath given me life" (33:4). "Thou sendest forth Thy Spirit, they are created: and Thou renewest the face of the earth" (Psalm 104:30).

God's word is spirit and life. There is power in God's word to set in motion events, and to bring to pass, the word that was spoken by those who have the authority to use it. God empowered mankind with this ability. Adam operated in this authority in the garden. When Adam stepped out of the will of God, which is the word of God, disobedience resulted. Disobedience is what caused this authority to become inactive and physical work to be required to set things in motion. Solomon, the wisest man to live, understood the power inherent in words.

> *Proverbs 18:21 "Death and life are in the power of the tongue; and they that love it shall eat the fruit thereof."*

The power of the tongue lies within the spoken word. Words can activate a death cycle or a life cycle. When words are spoke, the word, whether good or bad, will go into your future, create what you

MARRIAGE: WORK AND WARFARE

spoke and wait for you to arrive there for it to be carried out. If you do not like what is in your life today, look back to the words you spoke in the past. Those words framed your future, be it good or bad, death or life. Once you understand the power of words, begin to use them to change your life into what you want it to be. This will allow you to move from the toiling of physical labor, to speaking using the power of words and then to resting.

In the beginning, God rested from His work of creation after six days. Rest is important to God. He wants His people to enter into His rest. This rest is a rest from labor or physical activity to allow time for reflection and reliance on God. When one enters into God's rest, any work that is accomplished is through the being of man but through the power of God's Spirit working through man. Man's effort is at rest while God Spirit is at work. That is why Paul could say In Galatians 2:20 that he was crucified with Christ and that he no longer lived but Christ lived in him. There is no work being done by those who are crucified or dead.

When God presented the woman to Adam, God never instructed them to "work" at marriage. The only "work" man was given was to tend the garden. The only "work" the woman was given was to help Adam. There was no "work" required to be one flesh. Oneness and unity was inherent in their creative being.

Once sin entered, the oneness with God was disrupted and unity of the marriage relationship was damaged. In Genesis 3 we have a record of Adam accusing the woman and the woman accusing the serpent. Neither Adam nor his wife wanted to take responsibility for their actions or the actions of their spouse. Where they were once one flesh, we see them separating themselves from each other in their responsibility and accountability before God. This separation between Adam and the woman is the direct result of them being separated from God through sin.

Chapter 2 – The Work of Marriage

It is common in western culture to hear people say that "marriage is hard work". "A healthy marriage relationship takes work on the part of both the husband and wife." We see a struggle in relationships first manifested in Adam accusing God about the woman he was given. Then we see division between brothers Cain and Able that resulted in murder.

Today, all relationships require effort on the part of both spouses in the areas of communication, intimacy and oneness. We will explore the effects work has on each of these areas in marriage: The Work of Communication, The Work of Intimacy and The Work of Oneness.

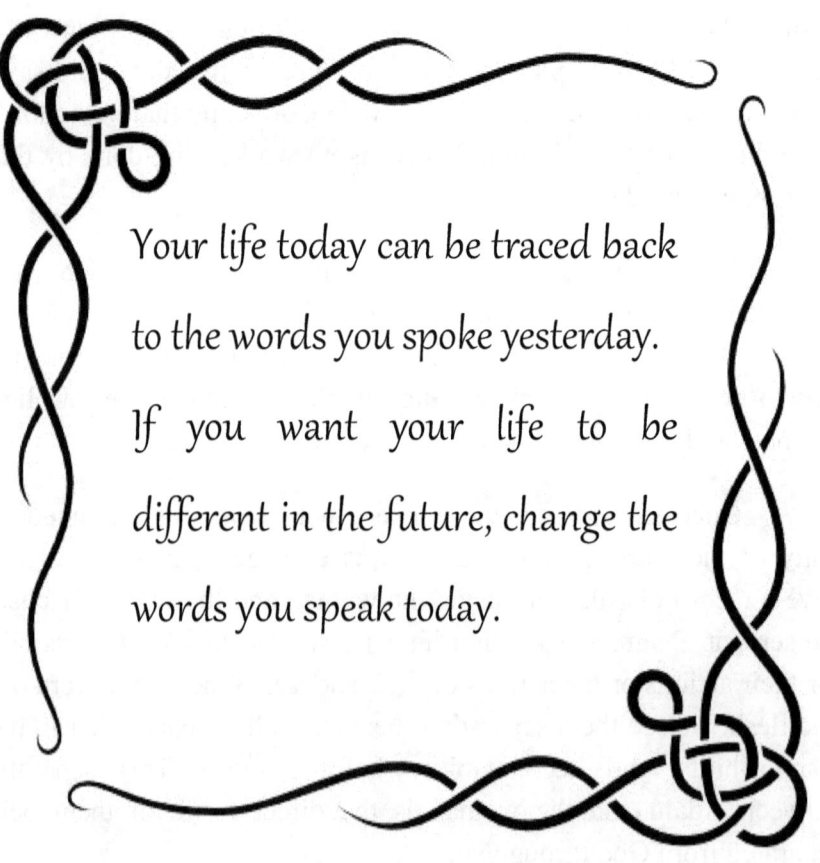

Your life today can be traced back to the words you spoke yesterday. If you want your life to be different in the future, change the words you speak today.

Marriage: Work and Warfare

Study Questions

1) Define work.

2) Are you and your spouse working towards a healthy marriage? How?

3) Work in the garden was not physical but verbal. What words are you speaking that work against your marriage?

4) What words are you speaking that work to improve your marriage?

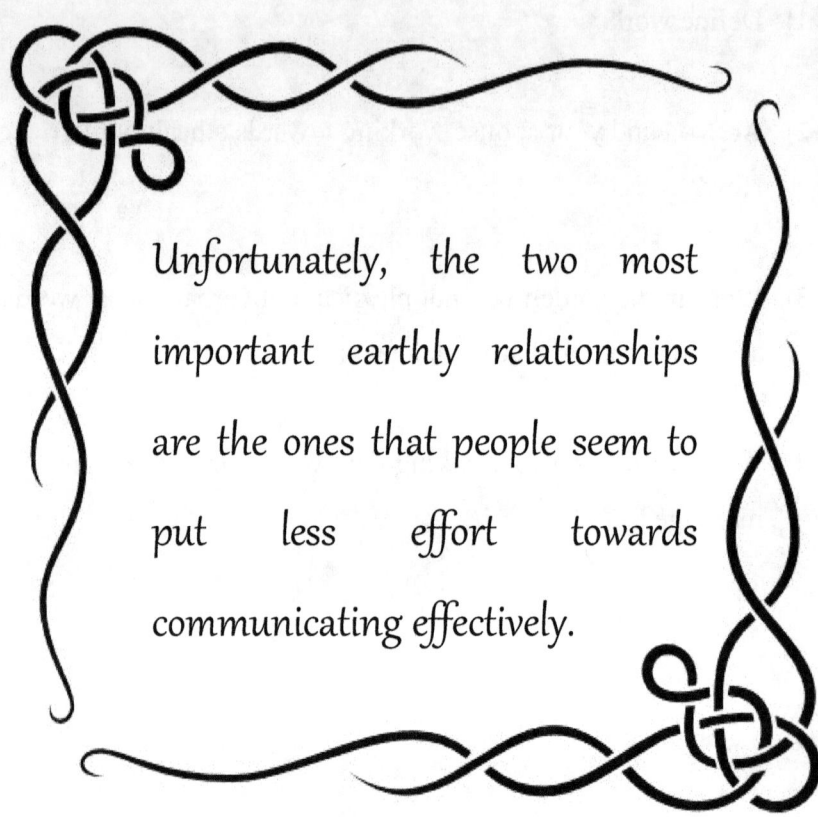

Unfortunately, the two most important earthly relationships are the ones that people seem to put less effort towards communicating effectively.

CHAPTER 3
THE WORK OF COMMUNICATION

In the beginning there was only one language. There was no communication barrier in the garden. God and man communicated perfectly. Man and woman communicated perfectly. The breakdown came when the subtle serpent began to communicate with woman. The serpent came with a different line of communication that challenged the perfect communication that existed.

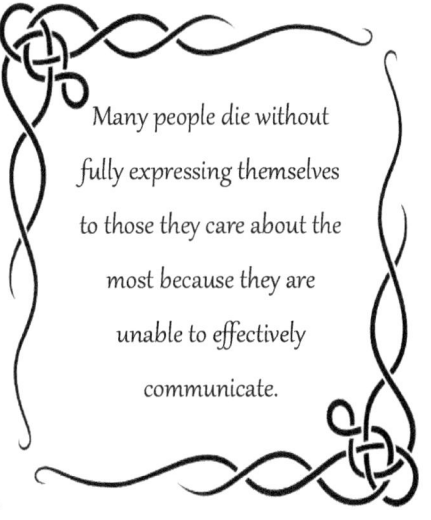

Many people die without fully expressing themselves to those they care about the most because they are unable to effectively communicate.

It was different because its source was not love, but deception. If the serpent came with the same communication that was already shared with God, man and woman, there would be no sin. It was sin because it caused the woman and man to miss the mark God had established for them. Communication that was well understood between God, man and woman changed with the introduction of sin. The sin nature is what makes it difficult for people to communicate. Now it takes effort or work for spouses to understand one another. It takes effort for man to communicate with God and with one another.

Effective communication requires work. We must put effort into understanding one another. When there is a breakdown in communication, then thoughts, intentions, ideas and passions are left unexpressed or misunderstood. Many people die without fully expressing themselves to those they care about the most because they are unable to communicate effectively.

Chapter 3 – The Work of Communication

God created each person different physically, with a different personality and most importantly, with their own will. Because we are all free-will agents, we have a choice in how we communicate and relate to others. The most effective communicators have mastered not only how to say what they mean, but also how to translate it with a language style that is understood by those with whom they are communicating.

People understand that it is important to work at effective communication on their jobs. Those who value friendships put effort into effectively communicating with their friends. The most important relationship on earth is the marriage relationship. The next most important relationship is that of family. Unfortunately, the two most important earthly relationships are the ones that people seem to put less effort towards communicating effectively. Spouses and other family members are often taken for granted. They are expected to understand, cope with and overlook ineffective communication. Yes, the more you know someone, fewer words may need to be used to express oneself, but those words should be ones others can relate to. Love covers a multitude of sins, even when it involves communication.

There are five keys that will help people communicate more effectively, if practiced. The five keys to communication (from the book Favor in Marriage by Akinyemi Adegbayi) are to listen attentively, do not interrupt, show interest, know how to ask questions and know when to ask questions.

࿇ Listen Attentively ࿇

When you listen attentively, you will be able to understand what your spouse is trying to communicate in their conversation. Believe it or not, when we listen, we may be able to understand what is being said, and ultimately find the answers while listening.

Listening attentively will lead to us being sympathetic to our spouse. When someone is speaking, we should make every effort to listen without distractions. Sometimes distractions are unavoidable. When the subject communicated is of high importance and urgency to the communicator, the more we should limit interruptions. For instance, if one person wants to talk about the possibility of losing their job and decisions that they need to soon make, they may not feel heard if the listener is on the phone, watching television or doing something that is of little immediate importance to the communicator. If instead the listener stops everything and looks interestingly at the person speaking, their body language communicates listening and that what the speaker is saying is being heard.

ஒ Do Not Interrupt ஒ

Interruption may show a lack of caring or that you are insensitive to what your spouse is saying. When you interrupt, the speaker may feel that what you are saying is more important to you than hearing than the message they want to share. Your spouse may think that you do not care or you do not want to hear what they are saying. Interruptions may break your spouse's train of thought and cause friction. When interrupted, your spouse may refuse to communicate further because what they are saying is not valued. When what someone is communicating is not valued, over time the communicator may not believe they are valued. Thus, the relationship is affected.

ஒ Show Interest ஒ

Interest is shown with non-verbal as well as verbal indicators. Non-verbal communication is expressed through movements, eye contact, facial expressions and other body language. Verbal communication clues, like tone, words and voice inflection let the

Chapter 3 – The Work of Communication

speaker know that the listener is following what is being said. These indicators will let your spouse know that you are interested. Therefore, your spouse may feel free to express more of what is on their hearts and mind. You may not necessarily agree with what they are saying, but be interested that they want to communicate with you. The alternative is for your spouse to not communicate with you or worse, share what they want to tell you to someone else.

❧ Know How to Ask Questions ☙

When you listen attentively without interruption and show interest in what is being said, you will know how to ask the correct questions. Questions will give you more information to help you communicate effectively in line with what the speaker is trying to communicate. Before you answer a question, repeat the question to confirm that your answer is to the same question that was asked. Your spouse may ask. "What would you like to eat tonight?" If you answer, "We have to meet Sandy's teacher tonight at 7:00 p.m." Your answer is important, but did not address the question. You may have heard "What do you want to do tonight?" instead of "What would you like to eat tonight?" If you would have repeated the question you heard, your spouse would have confirmed or corrected the question you thought you heard. Also, collect data from the conversation to ask questions that will lead the speaker to the answers they need. For example, "You mentioned that you bought fish last week. I would like to eat that tonight."

❧ Know When to Ask Questions ☙

A good question at the wrong time can create an explosion instead of quieting a storm. The wise author of Proverbs 25:11 explains that a word fitly spoken are like apples of gold in pictures of silver. Apples are fruit with many seeds. Once the fruit is used for nourishment, the seeds can be planted to harvest more fruit with more seeds. Gold and silver are both precious metals that have value in most cultures. A word spoken at the right time will nourish the soul whose seeds, when planted will bring innumerable harvests. Its value is precious cross-culturally. As you practice these tools, it will become easy to know when to ask questions.

Chapter 3 – The Work of Communication

STUDY QUESTIONS

1) What are the five keys to effective communication?

2) Evaluate yourself in each of the keys.
    a. What areas are you effective?
    b. What areas are you ineffective?
    c. How can you improve you communication skills?

3) Evaluate your spouse in each of the keys.
    a. What areas are your spouse effective?
    b. In what are examples of your spouse's ineffective communication?
    c. What can you do to lovingly assist your spouse to improve communication?

4) Commit to pray for both you and your spouse to have effective communication.

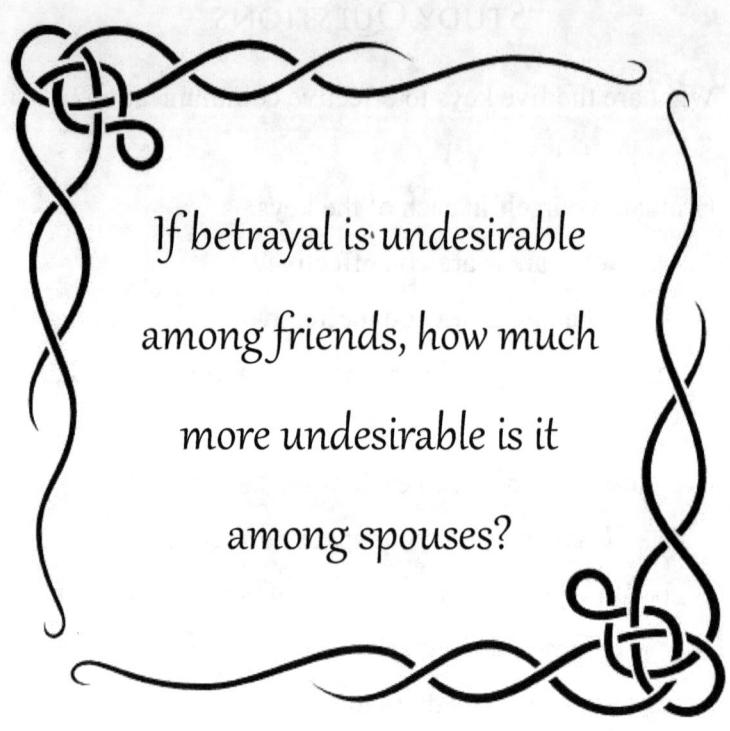

If betrayal is undesirable among friends, how much more undesirable is it among spouses?

CHAPTER 4
THE WORK OF INTIMACY

Intimacy is a close relationship of a personal nature. This can be sexual or non-sexual. Intimacy requires exposure of self, that is, one's heart and innermost being. There are different levels of intimacy. As we begin to reveal who we are, layers of protective covers that hide who we truly are will be removed. If a person is not willing to become vulnerable to another, intimacy will never take place. There will only be a surface interaction, if any interaction at all. Intimacy comes with trust, confidentiality, self-exposure, unconditional acceptance and time.

For many years I kept people at a distance, especially men. I chose to separate myself from certain types of people to get closer to God. Although I did get closer to God, God's heart is relationships. God only separates us from things and people who compete with his relationship with us. Otherwise, God wants us to be relational.

My husband is very relational. He never meets a stranger. He makes everyone feel as if they have known him for a long time. I had to adjust to this and be comfortable with who he is and allow him to get to know me past the surface. This was not easy, but he was patient. It took time for me to trust that as I exposed myself to him, I would not be rejected, hurt or exposed to others.

To increase intimacy in your marriage there are areas where work may be needed on the part of one or both spouses. The areas are trust, confidentiality, self-exposure, unconditional acceptance and time. Problems in any one or all of the following areas may affect the ability of a couple to experience intimacy and truly becoming one flesh.

Chapter 4 – The Work of Intimacy

✤ Trust ✤

Trust is a highly valued commodity in relationships. When spouses do not trust, then words, motives and actions are questioned. Trust is not instantaneous, but is developed over time. If you have been wounded, offended or wronged and no longer trust your spouse, repentance by the offending spouse and forgiveness by the offended spouse whether forgiveness is asked for or not, are initial steps that can begin to restore trust. Unless there is a change in behavior from the offending spouse, the offended spouse may never have complete trust in the marriage. Words, motives and actions affect trust in any relationship.

WORDS. When a person does not trust what their spouse says, they may seek other ways to ensure what their spouse says comes to past. Some will give up on the marriage. Some will compensate in other ways. In other words, the untrusting spouse may have to work at developing a backup plan just in case what their spouse said does not come to past. When there is trust in relationships, there is less work that is required to maintain the relationship. If your spouse has lost trust in what you say, begin to rebuild their trust by keeping your words. Do not say words you do not mean. Do not make promises you cannot keep. It may be difficult initially, but the rewards will be worth the work invested.

MOTIVES. The same is true when motives are questioned. When motives are not trusted, one person does not believe that the other person has their best interest at heart. This makes the person who does not trust feel vulnerable. Vulnerability leads to self-defense. Self-defense leads to protecting oneself from someone whom they should trust to protect them. If your spouse questions your motives and actions, began to bring down the wall of self-defense by becoming self-less towards them.

Actions. I have heard the saying, "Actions speak louder than words." If this is true, a person's actions that does not line up with what is being said can cause distrust even when their words seem trustworthy. This leads to confusion. Should actions be trusted over words?

> *Luke 6:45 "A good man out of the good treasure of his heart bringeth forth that which is good; and an evil man out of the evil treasure of his heart bringeth forth that which is evil: for of the abundance of the heart his mouth speaketh."*

Unless there is an underlying mental illness or addiction, a person's words generally line up with their actions.

> *Proverbs 18:21 "Death and life are in the power of the tongue: and they that love it shall eat the fruit thereof."*

Theses scriptures conclude that actions are the result of what is in a person's heart and mouth. When a person's words are contradicting their actions, trust their actions. Words are a cheap investment. Actions take more effort to manifest. Spouses, if your actions are not the true manifestation of your heart's desire towards your mate, change your actions.

ꙮ Confidentiality ꙮ

One of the worst actions among friends is betrayal. Betrayal is when someone you trust, use what they know to harm you. If betrayal is undesirable among friends, how much more undesirable is it among spouses? The spousal relationship is a covenant. One of the

Chapter 4 – The Work of Intimacy

characteristics of a covenant is that each party would give their lives to protect the other. Even to the point of death.

Spouses should trust that what they share is held in confidence by their mate. Except when it is a matter of life and death, spouses should hold confidential matters secret. The law of the United States of America recognizes the confidentiality of the spousal relationship. Spouses are not forced to testify against one another in court.

In Proverbs 31, Solomon describes a virtuous woman as one who will do her husband good not evil, all the days of her life. This means that even after the husband dies, the wife will keep the husbands character is tact. The reverse is also true. Paul states that the husband should love his wife as Christ loves the church and gave himself for her. While Jesus is the savior of the wife's soul, the husband is the savior of the wife's body. The husband is to protect his wife. Husbands guard, guide and govern the household. These duties of a husband include the confidentiality of the spousal relationship.

Intimacy is not easy, it takes work. It takes work in marriage to keep the secrets of your spouse. Intimacy becomes easier when spouses know that what they expose to their mate is not going to be shared with others or used against them.

ෂ Self-Exposure ෂ

Spouses should be willing to expose themselves to one another. The relationship between man and woman in the beginning was described as them being "naked and not ashamed." This nakedness referred to physical nakedness, as well as spiritual nakedness. Adam was given instructions to "tend the garden." The woman was given to Adam as a help meet. There was no need to "hide" from God or "hide" from one another until sin entered. The sin nature of mankind is what created the need for "self-protection." Spouses will never have true intimacy as long as they hide or protect themselves from one another.

It takes work to expose oneself. It takes more work to cover oneself. Are you not experiencing the level of intimacy with your spouse that comes from self-exposure? If not, why? Do you truly want the intimacy in your spousal relationship that comes from self-exposure? What can you do to become more transparent with your spouse? What would you like your spouse to do so that you will be more comfortable exposing yourself to him or her?

❧ Unconditional Acceptance ❦

One characteristic of God is that He loves us unconditionally. This agape love is why he was able to send His only begotten Son to die for our sins (John 3:16). In the beginning, man had this same capacity to agape. When the woman was presented to man, he did not find fault in her. Adam accepted the woman and called her "bone of my bone and flesh of my flesh." He identified her as a part of himself. It was not until after the fall, that Adam found fault in Eve. When God asked Adam how he knew he was naked and asked if he had eaten of the tree he was told not to eat, he did not answer the question. Instead, he shifted the blame to the woman. Yes she gave the fruit to him, but Adam chose to eat of it. He is ultimately responsible for his family.

Before my husband and I married, we chose to do premarital counseling. This is my first marriage. My husband had previous marital experience with a negative outcome. We needed this counseling. It helped us both. One of the exercises was on unconditional love. As we completed the study, I realized that I was still developing in my agape love for him. I do not recommend this as a test, but I was mean and cold towards him during our courtship.

Chapter 4 – The Work of Intimacy

There were times when I was not sure if I should marry him. During this study of the love spouses should share, I discovered that he had mastered this area of unconditional love while I was still developing and most often, failing in it. Thank God he looked past my immaturity and confusion on this subject and demonstrated the love of God towards me that I had never experienced before. He looked beyond our present circumstances and saw what God could do with our future. His love towards me was not based upon how I looked, what I did or what I said. It is a love that originated and has its existence with him and by him in spite of me. We married and are both continuing to grow in the love of God towards each other.

Unconditional acceptance is not easy; it takes effort or work. This does not mean that spouses should not encourage the other to change in areas that are falling short of God's best for them. It also does not mean that the accepted spouse does not have consequences for their actions. Each spouse is responsible for his or her own actions. Unconditional acceptance creates a safe environment for change where spouses are comfortable with intimacy and trust which leads to oneness.

ಲ Time ನಿ

Time is a commodity that each person is given the same quantity of each day. Once this commodity is spent or exchange for something, it can never be redeemed. Unlike it is portrayed in movies, no one can turn back time to make a different choice. Your spouse does not have any more hours in a day than you do. Each is given twenty-four hours. How each one uses that time will determine the level of intimacy developed in the marriage.

Among all the things that vie for attention, i.e. work, responsibilities, children and other relationships, know that the order should be God first, spouse second. Just as spouses cannot spend the entire twenty-four hours every day ignoring people and responsibilities to be in the presence of God, they also cannot do the same with their spouse. Spouses should understand that through the marriage relationship, they should become one. This oneness does not eliminate the individuality of the spouses. In the midst of daily activities, spouses should take time for one another. This takes work.

To demonstrate to your spouse that you have time for them in the midst of all the busyness, do something that they would appreciate. A quick communication by phone, email, text or a note tucked in their daily supplies will remind them that they are important to you. It will also jog their memory of you perhaps during a sensitive time when they need support. During the day, my husband and I communicate often. If one of us is busy, the other will text or call. This lets the other know that we are thought of. Find something that works for your specific relationship. Not something that causes your spouse to feel badgered or untrusted, but loved.

Effort should be made on each spouse's part to spend quality time together. When the time factor of marriage is ignored or taken for granted, intimacy suffers.

Chapter 4 – The Work of Intimacy

Marriage: Work and Warfare

Study Questions

1) Do you trust your spouse? Does your spouse trust you?

2) What can you do to increase the trust level in your marriage?

3) Has betrayal affected your marriage? What can you do to restore confidentiality?

4) Are you experiencing the level of intimacy you desire in your marriage?

5) Does your spouse agree with you? Why or Why not?

6) Study I Corinthians 13:4-8. Evaluate yourself and your spouse in each characteristic of love.

7) Pray for you and your spouse to be strengthen in the areas of both of your weaknesses. Accept areas where you fall short. Repent. Choose to change.

8) Are you too busy to enjoy your marriage? Schedule a set time with your spouse that you keep no matter what comes up.

Chapter 4 – The Work of Intimacy

MARRIAGE: WORK AND WARFARE

❧ CHAPTER 5 ❦
THE WORK OF ONENESS

How can two people become one flesh? It is not physically possible to become one with another human without sexual intercourse. We are three part beings: spirit, soul and body. Although all three parts are involved in every sex act, the physical aspect of sex is the lowest level of oneness. The spiritual aspect of sex is the highest level of oneness and is a picture of the worship between Man and God. The body obeys our spirit man or soul man, the one who is strongest. Two people can physically become one through sexual intercourse and never met again. The physical contact can be of short duration and may never happen again. The spirit and soul connection that takes place is more sublime and effects last longer. The oneness that takes place between souls and spirits is more difficult to separate than the physical. These connections are body to body tie, soul to soul tie and spirit to spirit tie. These ties between husband and wife are legal and ordained by God. When these ties are formed outside of the marriage covenant, they are illegal and can be exploited by Satan.

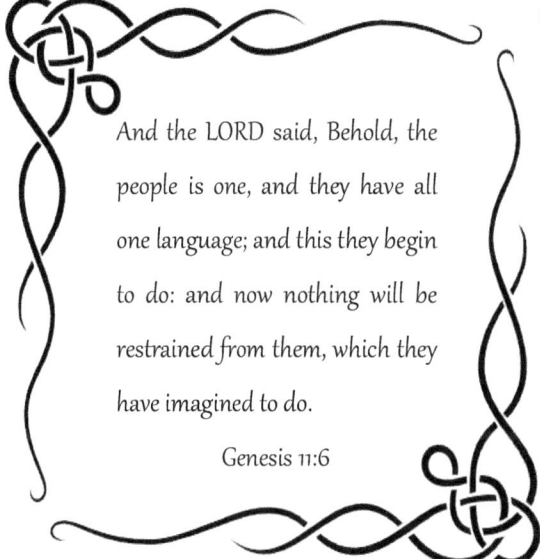

And the LORD said, Behold, the people is one, and they have all one language; and this they begin to do: and now nothing will be restrained from them, which they have imagined to do.

Genesis 11:6

In Genesis 11:6, Moses writes that nothing that people who are one, or in agreement, IMAGINE to do will be restrained or impossible. This is the power of agreement or the power of oneness. To become one or agree, two people must first work to find common

Chapter 5 – The Work of Oneness

ground not only in the body to body tie, but also in language, purpose, understanding and place on the level of soul to soul and spirit to spirit tie. For total oneness to take place, spouses must work towards oneness in these areas.

❧ Language ❧

Language is a form of communication. As described in the chapter on Communication, it takes work to communicate. Language is not just referring to country of origin or dialect, but also refers to agreement. Two people can speak the same language of a specific country and not agree with one another. For spouses to have one language, they must agree or speak the same thing from the heart regarding matters. It is like a double-minded person. For example, one spouse cannot say, "We are out of debt, in the name of Jesus." While the other spouse is constantly speaking, "We are not out of debt. You know what bills we have to pay. How can you say we are out of debt?" The two are speaking two different things about the same matter. They have two languages regarding their debt. When they agree in words and actions toward their debt being resolved, being out of debt will no longer be restrained from them. It will become a reality.

Spouses, seek to use the power of agreement to the benefit of your marriage. Things that were impossible will be easy to accomplish. Things will happen quicker, not only because you have the agreement or support of your spouse, but also, God will be in the midst to bring it to pass when it lines up with His word.

❧ Purpose ❧

Solomon writes in Ecclesiastes 4:9-12, *"Two are better than one, for they have a good reward for their labor. For if they fall, one* *will lift up his fellow, but woe to him who is **alone** when he falleth; for he hath not another to **help** him up."* Notice he used the words "alone" and "help." God describe Adam without the woman as "alone." He also used the word "help" to describe his purpose for woman. The creative purpose for woman was so that the man was not alone and to provide help. The wise writer understood the power of agreement in purpose just as our creator intended. When two work towards the same goal, they will have a good reward for their labor. When difficult times come, they can rely on one another for help.

This is true for spouses. Spouses should have a single purpose. They have each other to encourage, understand point of reference, and strengthen one another while fulfilling their purpose. When spouses are working towards differing or opposing purposes, division arises. This division leads to separate lives and the marriage bond is weakened. Spouses will feel like they are alone in their pursuit. They will not have the strength of the relationship to help during difficult times. What one purpose are you and your spouse working towards fulfilling? If you do not know the purpose of your marriage or have developed a different purpose from that of your spouse, both spouses should come together and seek God's purpose for your marriage and work towards it.

❧ Understanding ☙

Two people can have the same teachings, experiences and cultural background, but view them differently. This is because character, personality and motives individualize each teaching, experience and cultural background. Discuss with your spouse your views of things that are important to you and to them.

There are some areas where it is not as important for you to have the same understanding or agreement. It is important, however, to understand things the way your spouse understands them, even if

Chapter 5 – The Work of Oneness

you do not agree. This understanding of your spouse's view will help you to find common ground and agreement on issues that are important.

All battles do not have to be fought. All conflicts do not have a winner. There are some battles that are best left unfought and some conflicts where no one wins. When the stakes are high and the spoils too great, remember that you are on the same team and want to share the victories together, not as opponents.

In Matthew 5:25 we are admonished to agree with our adversary quickly, before the disagreement escalates to involve the courts and debts result in prison terms. It may seem extreme to relate this scripture to spouses, but the principle of finding common ground to agree does relate to marriage. Spouses should view disagreements as something that could rip the fabric of their lives apart if allowed to fester and not be kept in proper perspectives. Is your position on the matter of more importance than your marital relationship? If not, find common ground to agree and move on. The possibility of what can be lost is not worth the cost.

ꙮ Place (Geographical Area) ꙮ

Oneness is difficult to achieve when two people live in different geographical areas. To experience oneness, spouses should make every effort to live in a single place. The marital relationship may sustain for a season, but being in different locations for extended periods of time strains any marriage.

This is evident in military marriages. Because the military requires spouses to separate for months and years at a time, many succumb to adultery and or end in divorce. No matter how much spouses communicate through writing, phone calls, or even video calls, there are events and occurrences that are missed that can never be communicated. There are some emotions that cannot be expressed through words. There are fears that cannot be calmed without a touch. There is a silent support that comforts just by being physically there. When opportunities are missed, even with a valid excuse, the marriage bond suffers. The spouses become vulnerable and temptation can creep in. It is not a matter of whether loves still exists between the spouses. It is not about the lack of love, but the absence of presence.

Very few marriages survive the strain of distance. It takes, not only love, but commitment, a common purpose and the power of forgiveness for this type of marriage to survive. If your marriage is going through a season where distance is necessary because of work, school, citizenship or even incarceration, the power of God is able to sustain the marriage. As soon as possible and as often as you can, be reunited physically, for the sake of the marriage.

Be careful of the counsel you receive regarding your marriage. Guard your marriage bond and your spouse from the opinions of those not in your situation. Also, be on guard from those who have had a long distance marriage that failed. Your marriage is not theirs. Their circumstances are not yours. You are not them and your spouse is not theirs. Your marriage is uniquely yours. Do all that you can to make your marriage one that is strong and one that last for the rest of your life.

I have counseled with spouses who have walked though this difficult time of separation. The knowledge that this separation was temporary and had a definite time frame helped eased some of the strain. Still there were times when the enemy tried to cause reason for divorce. Faith in God, love of spouse, reason for separation, children and time of separation all weighed heavily in the decision to stay in the marriage. The greatest of these being faith in God's Word and love. That is, being one with God and one with each other.

Chapter 5 – The Work of Oneness

All battles do not have to be fought.

All conflicts do not have a winner.

There are some battles

that are best left unfought...

And some conflicts where no one wins.

Study Questions

1) Are you and your spouse truly one?

2) List the areas you and your spouse agree. i.e. Where to live, how to handle finances, beliefs, etc.

3) What are the areas where you are not in agreement, but would like to be? What are you willing to do to bring the change you desire?

4) Pray for God to empower you and your spouse to be one as Jesus and the Father are one according to John 17:11, 21

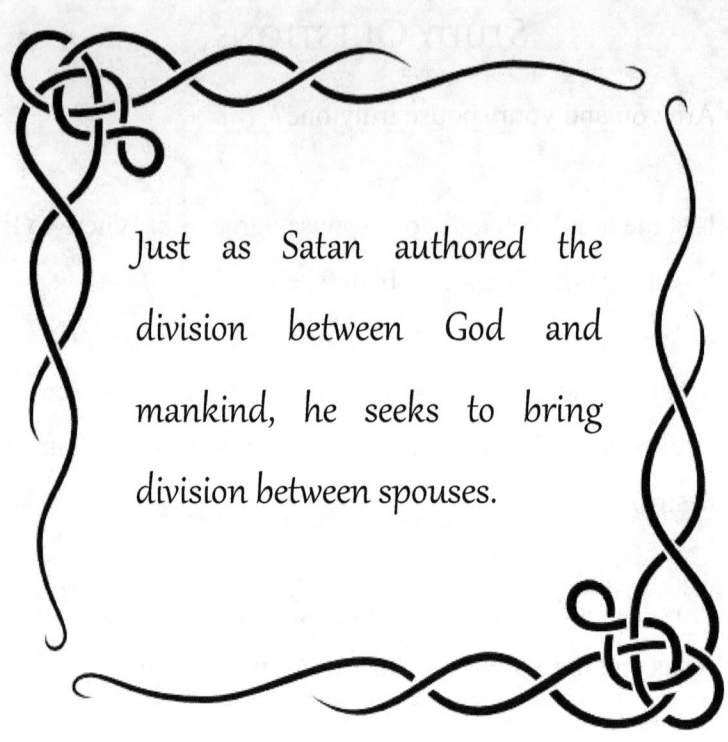

Just as Satan authored the division between God and mankind, he seeks to bring division between spouses.

CHAPTER 6
THE WARFARE OF MARRIAGE

If you are married and have not experienced warfare, you probably do not understand what spiritual warfare is. Every marriage is under attack. It is not because your marriage is not a healthy marriage, but because there is an enemy that seeks to destroy every marriage. The enemy is not your spouse, but Satan. Just as Satan brought division between God and mankind, he seeks to bring division between spouses. Paul in Ephesians describes the marriage relationship as an example or picture of the relationship between Christ and the church. When marriages are destroyed, the image or picture of the relationship between Christ and the church becomes distorted.

What does the picture of Christ and his bride, the church, look like? Jesus is the word that became flesh and lived among mankind. The word is truth, perfect and timeless. The church does not always represent truth, is not perfect and has limited time. Jesus laid down his divinity and was clothed with humanity so that he could restore the relationship between God and man that Adam lost. He did this by becoming the perfect sacrifice. His blood was offered once for all upon the mercy seat of heaven. He will return to earth once more and receive his bride into eternity.

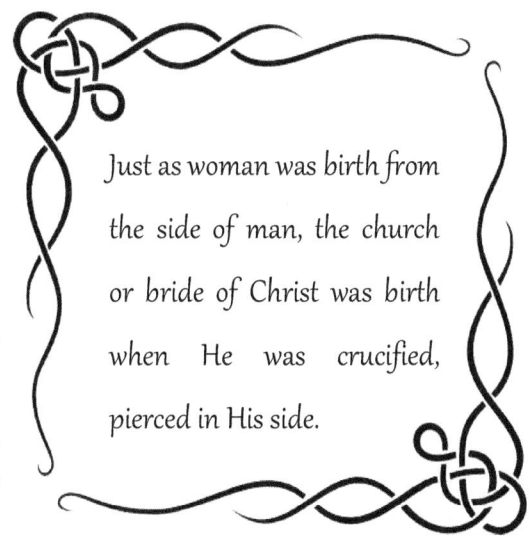

Just as woman was birth from the side of man, the church or bride of Christ was birth when He was crucified, pierced in His side.

Chapter 6 – The Warfare of Marriage

To get an idea of what this unlikely couple's photograph would look like, let's look at Hosea and Gomer. Hosea's name means savior. Gomer means complete. Ironically, she would not be what she was called, complete, until she accepted Hosea, her husband and savior. Hosea was a prophet to Israel. God used his life and marriage to demonstrate to Israel His love for them. God instructed Hosea to marry Gomer. It is not recorded that Hosea desired a wife. God chose him to marry Gomer, one who would be unfaithful so that when Israel looked at his marriage they would see a picture of their unfaithfulness to God. Unlike the church, Gomer did not pretend to be perfect. She did not condemn others for being different. Instead she struggled with her unfaithfulness while married to one who was faithful. Hosea was faithful to God and his wife, while Gomer was longing for her lovers. Time after time, she wondered away from her marriage covenant. Time after time, Hosea went after her as she went after other lovers. He raised offspring who did not have his blood. When her lovers sold her into slavery, it was Hosea, her savior, who paid the price for her freedom.

Christ is the same with the church. Just as woman was birth from the side of man, the church or bride of Christ was birth when He was crucified, pierced in his side. Just as Satan sowed discord between God and Adam and man and woman, he seeks to cause division between Christ and the church. This division is evident in the marriages or lack of marriages among believers.

Beloved, Satan has sinned from the beginning. He has much experience in dividing what should be indivisible. Do not be deceived. Your marriage is not immune from his plots of evil, but it can be protected from them because of the shed blood of Jesus. If one was to take a picture of Christ and His bride, would it resemble the picture of Hosea and Gomer? Or would the sinless one be one with a church without spot or wrinkle? Does your marriage reflect what the relationship of Christ and the church should be or does it look more like the husband, the wife, and other lovers? While putting the necessary work into your marriage for its success, do not be ignorant of the warfare against it. Guard your marriage against the warfare the enemy wages to destroy it.

Chapter 6 – The Warfare of Marriage

Marriage: Work and Warfare

Study Questions

1) Does your marriage reflect the intended example of Christ and the church?

2) Do others look at your marriage and desire the God your serve?

3) List attacks have you and your spouse overcome.

4) Use the knowledge of these victories to have confidence that you will overcome any future attacks together.

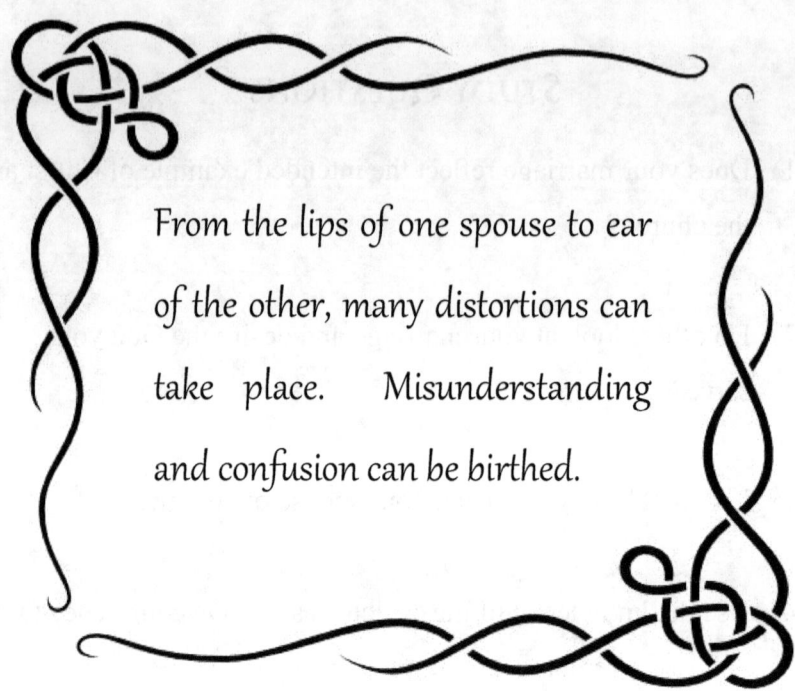

From the lips of one spouse to ear of the other, many distortions can take place.   Misunderstanding and confusion can be birthed.

CHAPTER 7
THE WARFARE OF COMMUNICATION

Communication is a vital part of all marriages. While the work of communicating in marriage is something that most couples can identify, the warfare of communication is not so evident. How many times have spouses had a conversation that was misunderstood? One spouse may say something that makes perfect sense to them, but to the other spouse it sounds foreign. Remember, Satan is called the prince of the air. He is also described as being the author of confusion. Words are spoken into the air. From the lips of one spouse to ear of the other, many distortions can take place. Misunderstanding and confusion is birthed. There are several things spouses can do to reduce communication failure.

Pray Together Daily

When couples pray together daily, it is a time for them to reset their compass so that each spouse knows where the other is going, doing and agree on the path for them to take. It also, invites God to be a part of their daily lives. A couple's daily prayer list can include: Prayer for the success of their marriage, their children, tasks or goals to achieve in business, ministry, etc., regarding the will of God for their lives.

PRAY FOR EACH OTHER DAILY. When couples pray for each other, it reconnects the heart strings. It takes the focus off of one's self and gives it to another. It is difficult to be angry with someone whom you sincerely intercede for daily. This prayer should not be selfish, but selfless. It should be what is best for your mate, which in turn is best for you. Pray for their well-being, success on job, protection, wisdom, etc. Your spouse should be better because of you in their life. Do you bring out the best in your spouse? Do you ignite

Chapter 7 – The Warfare of Communication

or stir up the good that was lying dormant in them? Like Mary and Elizabeth, do the babes or dreams in you both leap when you come together? Does your spouse bring out the best in you?

❧ Regular Communion Together, At Home ☙

The early churches had no formal buildings. They met in the homes of believers. Communion was also partaken in homes. Today, spouses can take communion in their homes as well as corporately in their local church. As often as one takes communion, he remembers the Lord and demonstrates the Lord's death until he returns. When spouses do this they are fellowshipping with one another on the common ground of Jesus' birth, death and resurrection. When couples come together over the cup of communion, it causes them to evaluate their lives individually. As they discern correctly the Lord's body they can partake of the cup without the penalty of damnation, sickness and death. I Corinthians 11:23-32. Jesus Christ took upon him the sin of the mankind, so that we could be reconciled to God. Therefore, communion not only signifies salvation, but also reconciliation, peace, protection and healing. Isaiah 53

> "Do not assume your spouse hears what you said with the same understanding you have."

Remember, you and your spouse are becoming one flesh, but the individual persons that are coming together have different histories, experiences and environmental influences. Everyone hears through their own ears, not your ears. They see and perceive through their own experiences, not yours. It is an easy task to know for sure that person you are speaking to heard what you wanted to say, but often, this task is neglected. To verify, just ask them to repeat what they heard you say. Do not give up and ignore the fact that they did not get the understanding you desired. Be patient, and learn the art of communicating with the language your spouse understands.

ᚼ Walk in Love ᚽ

There are four different words for love in the Greek language. *Agape* is unconditional love. The other three are conditional. *Storge* is familial love between parent and child. *Phileo* is brotherly love. *Eros* is sensual or romantic attraction. Unfortunately, the English language groups all these types into one word: Love. This is why the word "love" is abused and misunderstood in Western communications. When someone says "I love you" what do they mean? Are they saying, "I agape you?" Do they mean they "phileo" you? Or are they simply attracted to you sexually? To understand agape love we must look to the One who IS Love, God. I Corinthians 13:4-7, Love is patient, kind, not envious, not rude, not boastful, not proud, not selfish, not easily angered, it does not rejoice in evil but rejoices in good. It always hopes, always trust, always preservers.

LOVE NEVER FAILS.

God is love. *I John 3:7-13 "Beloved, let us love one another; for love is of God; and every one that loveth is born of God, and knoweth God. 8 He that loveth not knoweth not God; for God is love. 9 In this was manifested the love of God toward us, because that God sent his only begotten Son into the world, that we might live through him. 10 Herein is love, not that we loved God, but that he loved us, and sent his Son to be the propitiation for our sins. 11 Beloved, if God so loved us, we ought to also love one another. 12 No man hath seen God at any time. If we love one another, God dwelleth in us, and his love is perfected in us. 13 Hereby know we that we dwell in him, and he in us, because he hath given us of his Spirit."*

Chapter 7 – The Warfare of Communication

If you have not truly demonstrated agape love towards your spouse, make a decision to start today. This type of love is not dependent on the actions of your spouse. It has its origin with you and is only dependent upon you. Ask God, through the power of His Holy Spirit to empower you to practice the God kind of love towards your spouse and others. Evaluate yourself. Study I Corinthians 13:4-7. Each characteristic of love, study it. Decide to put each into action. Expect change, not only in your own life, but also the lives of those you love.

❧ Walk in Forgiveness ❧

Matthew 6:12, 14-15 "And forgive us our debts, as we forgive our debtors. 14 For if ye forgive men their trespasses, your heavenly Father will also forgive you: 15 But if ye forgive not men their trespasses, neither will your heavenly Father your trespasses."

Forgiveness is a matter of life and death, your being forgiven or condemned. You may live beyond the death of the one you choose to continue to hold guilty, but the quality of your life will be as if you are dying slowly spiritually. Free yourself by freeing others. Your forgiving others frees God to forgive you.

No offense, injustice or injury is worth holding the offender in bondage. You cannot hold another guilty and you be freed from the penalty of your wrongs. Your unwillingness to forgive anyone will affect your marriage relationship. Being unforgiving opens the door for bitterness, anger, resentment, oppression, depression, possession and even murder. If there is someone you have been unwilling to forgive, I pray that you will release them and forgive them of the wrong. This in turn will release you.

Marriage: Work and Warfare

> *"Do not believe the words of others before you believe the words of your spouse."*

Your spouse is to be your number one ally. Although you have known and trusted others before your marriage vows, now it is time to forsake all others and cling to your spouse. This includes giving your spouse the benefit of the doubt, until facts are known.

Trust takes time and is earned. You and your spouse must be a unified front. If one spouse allows the words of others to be believed above the other spouse's words, this sows a wedge of division between spouses. It will also lead to insecurity, self-defense and self –preservation in the other spouse.

In situations where you may doubt the veracity of your spouse, discuss it with your spouse privately and come to a conclusion to agree or disagree, not publicly. Public confrontation is not pleasant and can inflict damage on a marriage that may take years to overcome. Whether your spouse is wrong or right, stand with your spouse and lovingly shed light on what you believe to be truth. When spouses argue publicly or disagree publicly, it may cause shame and an uncomfortable situation for one or both spouses. As much as possible, we should walk in love with your spouse and others.

Chapter 7 – The Warfare of Communication

Marriage: Work and Warfare

Study Questions

1) Pray specific prayers for your spouse, marriage and family.

2) Are you a better person because of the presence of your spouse in your life?
    a. If so, thank your spouse and let them know how they have influenced your life. If not, why?

3) If you and your spouse are believers in Jesus as your Lord and savior, begin to take communion at home. Take notice of how you handle the activities of the day. Is your behavior different? Do you notice peace? Are you better connected to your spouse?

4) Taking communion regularly is a small investment that will reap many benefits for generations to come.

5) It is difficult to take communion with your spouse when there is anger or unresolved offences. Humble your self, repent and be reunited with God and your spouse. 2 Chronicles 7:1

Chapter 8 – The Warfare of Intimacy

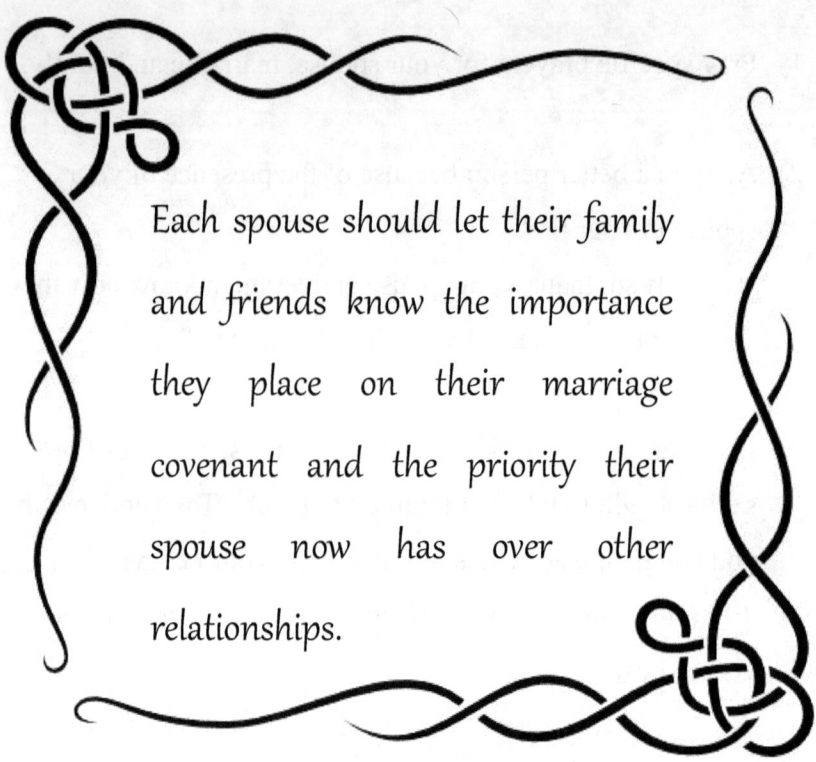

Each spouse should let their family and friends know the importance they place on their marriage covenant and the priority their spouse now has over other relationships.

Chapter 8
The Warfare of Intimacy

As stated previously, guard your marriage relationship. This is the most important earthly relationship. God chose the marital relationship to represent how He relates to the church. The marital relationship takes priority over the relationship each spouse has with their children, parents, siblings and friends. Therefore, it must be protected. There are several things spouses can do to safe guard their marriage from outside forces and protect intimacy.

Protect the Marriage Covenant

In a marriage covenant, two become one. This covenant is sealed with blood and enforceable until the death of a spouse. This is why God hates divorce and only permitted it through Mosaic Law because of the hardness of man's heart.

> *Mark 10:5-9 "And Jesus answered and said unto them, For the hardness of your heart he wrote you this precept. 6 But from the beginning of the creation God made them male and female. 7 For this cause shall a man leave his father and mother, and cleave to his wife; 8 And they twain shall be on flesh; so then they are no more twain, but one flesh. 9 What therefore, God has joined together, let no man put asunder."*

To protect your marriage covenant, do not share intimate details of your marriage with others unless it is a life and death situation. If a spouse is being abused or pressured to commit or support unlawful acts, help and counsel from others may be

Chapter 8 – The Warfare of Intimacy

necessary. There are situations when professional help is necessary and should be sought. When counseling is necessary it is best, if possible, that both spouses participate in the counseling sessions. Outside of these situations, I do not advise that spouses invite others to impose their opinion about your marriage or spouse. Remember, the outsiders are not privy to all details and are only hearing part of the story. Once you invite them into your marriage, they may expect you to respond to situations the way they would. When you chose a different course of action and have reconciled with your spouse, they may harbor resentment.

Remember, others do not have the grace or patience given to you by God for your marriage. Many times friends and family mean well, but do they have the best interest of your marriage relationship at the heart of their words and actions? Usually friends and family hold only one spouse's interest at heart. It may be necessary to share some things about your spouse or marriage with trained professionals. Be discerning, use wisdom and most of all, remain prayerful about with whom and what you share.

❧ Leave and Cleave ☙

The man was instructed in Genesis to leave his father and mother and cleave to his wife. Severing the parent-child bond to establish the husband-wife bond is of utmost importance. As long as either spouse holds their relationship with their parents as primary above the relationship with their spouse, intimacy in the marriage will never be complete. This severing process takes time and is not immediate. However, each spouse should let their family know the importance they place on their marriage covenant and the priority of their spouse. Once this is done, much unnecessary warfare that comes to divide spouses will be eliminated and intimacy in marriage will be strengthened.

Marriage: Work and Warfare

This can also apply to the parent-child relationship of a spouse who has children outside of the current marriage. Children, especially adult children, should not be held in higher esteem than one's spouse.

If you have given your family, either parent or child, more importance than your spouse you have not obeyed God's instruction to leave and cleave to your spouse. I encourage you to repent. Ask God and your spouse to forgive you. Begin to make your marriage the most important human relationship on earth.

❧ Maintain an Undefiled Marriage Bed ☙

The Bible describes marriage as honorable and the marriage bed as undefiled. How can a marriage bed be defiled? The marriage bed is the place of covenant. The marriage covenant is established and maintained through sexual intimacy. Every time a couple has sexual relations, the covenant is renewed. In the Old Testament, after the wedding night, the token of bloody sheets was proof of the virginity of the wife and established the marriage. In the United States court of law, a divorce is not granted unless the couple has refrained from sexual relations for ninety days. The sexual relationship in marriage is respected by courts of law. How much more should covenant people honor it? There are various things that can defile the marriage bed. Defile means to make unclean, to desecrate or make unholy.

Things That Defile the Marriage Bed

- **ADULTERY** – This involves sexual intimacy with someone who is not your spouse. When a spouse is involved in an adulterous relationship it breaks the marriage covenant. Although God hates divorce, Moses permitted divorce in the law because of the hardness

Chapter 8 – The Warfare of Intimacy

of man's heart. Many marriages have been reconciled after adultery, but it is Biblical grounds for divorce.

- **PORNOGRAPHY** – It's not just a problem for men. Women are increasingly admitting to addictive pornographic behaviors. Not only women, the industry has greater access to children and teenagers through technology. This is important because if a spouse has a problem, it probably begin before adulthood. This addictive entrapment is the depiction of erotic behavior intended to cause sexual excitement. This includes magazines, Internet media, movies, photographs, strip clubs, etc. Although physical contact may not take place, it causes mental images that invade one's mind and build fantasies that the spouse is not able to compete with.

If you or your spouse is attracted to pornography, deliverance and or counseling may be needed to break free and to restore the marriage bond. Pornography is a gateway to adultery and perversion and decreases intimacy in the marriage. Do not allow it to destroy your life and your family. The first step to being free from pornography is to repent and renew your mind with the Word of God. Begin to memorize scripture that you can focus on when thoughts or urges try to take control of you. You are more powerful than the image that seeks to ensnare you. Take the thought captive according to II Corinthians 10:4-5.

- **ABUSE** – There are many types of abuse. Abuse can be physical, mental, social, verbal, financial, etc. Whatever type of abuse, it can cause one spouse to withdraw from the pleasure of the marriage bed. If you are the abuser, seek help to identify the source of your anger and learn to control it, instead of using it to control others. If you are the abused, pray for your spouse and do not stay in a life-threating situation. Get help. Remember, your spouse is not your enemy, but is being used by the enemy of our souls to destroy not only your marriage but your lives. Instead of warring with your spouse, both of you turn your attack to the one who deserves it. He is there to steal, kill and to destroy. Do not let him be victorious. He is a defeated foe. Believers must enforce his defeat and not give in.

- **CONVERSATIONS THAT CAUSE DIVISION.** Be careful of what conversations you discuss with your spouse at a time when your attention should be towards him or her. Conversations regarding previous relationships or comparing your spouse to others should not be discussed during the vulnerable time of bedtime intimacy. Use wisdom, discretion and keep a peaceful atmosphere in your home.

Things that Sanctify the Marriage Bed

- **PRAYER:** Prayer takes the focus off of the circumstances and situations and places the focus on God. Take time daily to pray with and for your spouse. The prayer can be short or long, but it should be from the heart. Pray can include success for the day's events, wisdom, strength, peace and unity in your family.

The prayer could also include declarations of what the Word of God says about you and your spouse: Heavenly Father, I thank you that my husband is mighty in you. He loves me just like Christ loves the church. He leads our family into truth with wisdom from above. He is a man of integrity. He has power over the power of the enemy, because greater is the one who is in him, Jesus, than the one who is in the world. We have sufficiency in all things. We don't worry about tomorrow because we know that you are Jehovah Jireh. You have seen ahead and have made provisions for us. Thank you in Jesus name amen.

A husband prayer could be: Heavenly Father, I thank you that my wife is blessed, healthy and strong in you. Protect her, guide her, watch over her and keep her safe from all harm. Give her wisdom and peace as she goes out and as she comes in. Thank you that she respects me as her husband and she is the perfect help for me. Thank you that she is secure because of my relationship with you and your provision for us. Our children rise up and call her blessed. In the name of Jesus, Amen.

- **COMMUNION:** When communion was first instituted, the church met in the homes of believers. Because we now have specific buildings labeled "church" sometimes we forget that the church is not just a corporate group of people that meet in a building, but the church is really the people. We are "temple" or "church" of the Holy Spirit. Because of the price Jesus paid to reconcile us back to God, He now dwells in us. Paul describes this as a mystery: Christ in us, the hope of glory.

Therefore, we do not have to wait until we are in our local church among other believers with a pastor officiating this ordinance. We can partake of it in our homes. Communion causes one to take an inventory of our own life and invites the protection, healing, peace, reconciliation and salvation of Jesus. When families, especially spouses, take communion together in their homes, it protects them from attacks on their spirits, souls and bodies. It is a reminder of the stripes that Jesus bore for our healing and the cross he bore for our salvation. It reminds the enemy that we are no longer under his kingdom, but are sons of God, heirs and joint heirs with Christ. If you and your spouse do not take communion at home, begin to do it today.

My husband and I take communion on a regular basis. Sometimes we partake of it daily and sometimes weekly or monthly. For us, it is a time when we come together, take our eyes off our circumstances and both look to the cross. When we are under attack, our observance of this ordinance increases. When the attack is not as severe we tend to slowly decrease our frequency. When we take communion I am assured that my husband is looking to God for our direction, protection and provision. Intimacy is easier when we both are in tune with God. The most important thing is that you observe this ordinance. As often as you do, you remember Jesus Christ and what he did for us.

- **FORGIVENESS:**

    Matthew 6:14-15 "For if ye forgive men their trespasses, your heavenly Father will also forgive you: ^{15} But if ye forgive not men their trespasses, neither will your Father forgive your trespasses."

Forgiveness unifies and reconciles. Forgiving someone from an offence is more for the sake of the offended than the offender. Many times when someone is unable to forgive an offense, the wounds do not heal properly. It is like a broken leg that was not set and bound properly. Once healed, there is still evidence that the previous injury has a major impact in the daily life of the one who was wounded. They may be able to walk, but there is a limp that identifies that there was an injury.

This is the same with someone who moves past an offense without forgiving the offender. Some form of healing may have taken place that covers the wound, but deep inside, the injury was not properly dealt with. Evidence of an unforgiving heart cripples the offended and keeps them from the freedom they need. If your spouse or someone else has offended you, whether they have the strength to say, "I'm sorry" or not, make the choice to forgive them. There are marriages that suffer because of offenses their spouse experienced before they met. You may feel that you have the right to be offended, but do you have the right to be forgiven? Jesus explains that when we are not able to forgive others, God is limited in His ability to forgive us. Our not forgiving others hinders us from being forgiven.

What could any person, no matter how evil, no matter how much they deserve punishment, do that is worth you not being

Chapter 8 – The Warfare of Intimacy

forgiven? When we hold others guilty, God is not free to judge them. Forgive them, no matter what the offense, even if the offense resulted in death or worse than that, a life of suffering on earth. I do not know what you have experienced, but God does. He gave His Son to pay for the sins of the world. The sins of the world include not only the sins you have committed, but also the sins committed against you. They were paid for before the actual event took place. Therefore, forgive and you will be forgiven.

- **REPENTANCE:**

    I John 1:9 "If we confess our sins, he is faithful and just to forgive us our sins, and to cleanse us from all unrighteousness 2 Corinthians 7:10 For godly sorrow worketh repentance to salvation not to be repented of, but the sorrow of the world worketh death."

Repentance frees from guilt. Repentance is not just a feeling of regret, but a choice to change. Once true repentance takes place, the sin is forgiven and forgotten by God. You cannot make people forgive or forget an offensive act you have repented of, but repent anyway. You will be cleansed from every unrighteousness associated with the event. Are you ready to be cleansed? Repent.

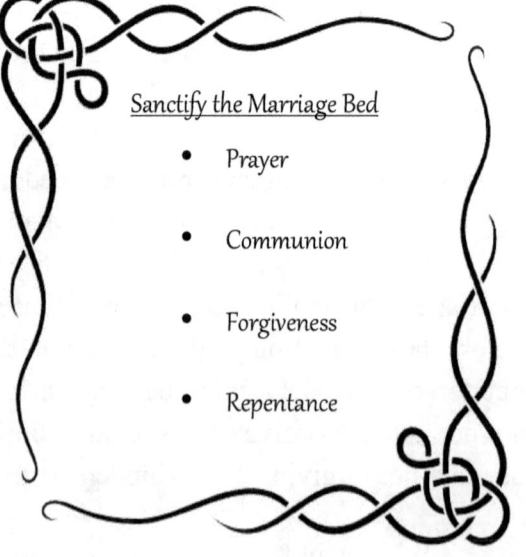

Sanctify the Marriage Bed

- Prayer
- Communion
- Forgiveness
- Repentance

STUDY QUESTIONS

1) Have there been times when you did not protect your marriage covenant? It may not be too late. Repent and ask God to give you wisdom to protect your marriage covenant.

2) Close any doors that you may have open that gives others access to or cause your spouse, home and family to be vulnerable.

3) Set boundaries around your marriage, spouse and family that protect them, but that do not hold them captive in a prison you build for them.

4) What are you willing to do sanctify your marriage bed and keep it holy?

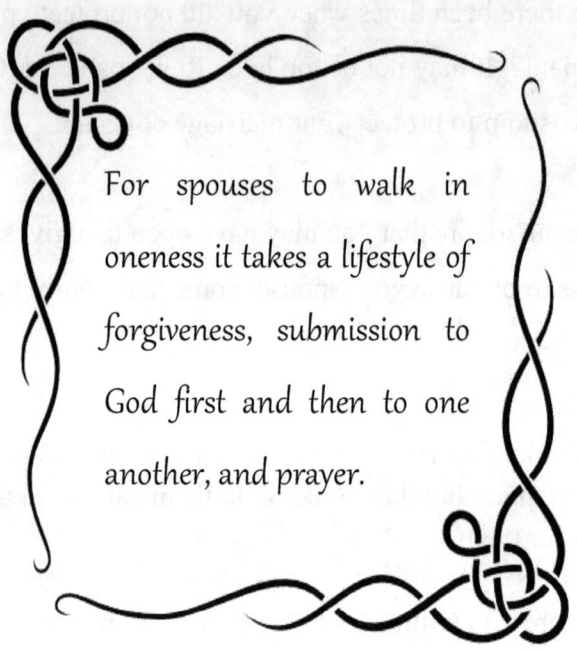

For spouses to walk in oneness it takes a lifestyle of forgiveness, submission to God first and then to one another, and prayer.

CHAPTER 9
THE WARFARE OF ONENESS

"For we wrestle not against flesh and blood, but against principalities, against powers, against spiritual wickedness in high places."

Ephesians 6:10

Jesus prayed that His followers would be one just as He and the Father are one in John 17. If it is God's heartfelt desire for His followers to be one, how much more does God desires oneness with spouses? This oneness in the body of Christ is to reflect the oneness in the God Head. The oneness in the marriage relationship is to reflect the oneness between Christ and the church. When we look at the lack of unity within the body of Christ, we will understand the lack of oneness in the marriages of those within the body of Christ.

This is why so many Christian leaders are falling in their marriages. There is an increase of divorce among pastors and other Christian leaders. This discord among the brethern is a direct attack from the enemy. God is not the author of discord among believers and in fact hates it. Proverbs 6:19b

For spouses to walk in oneness it takes a lifestyle of forgiveness, submission to God first and then to one another, and prayer. Both spouses must realize that what is seen is not the real world. What is not seen, that which is spiritual, is the real world. Do not be deceived by what you see. We are spirit, the only part of man that can connect with God. We have a soul, which is our intellect, will and emotions. Both spirit and soul live in a physical body. Our body is what allows us to legally interact in the physical world. The true person is not the body that we see physically, but the spirit man who has been regenerated by the resurrected Christ if we have

Chapter 9 – The Warfare of Oneness

accepted Him. If one has not accepted Jesus Christ as their savior, know that that person has not been regenerated and is living life based upon their soul man.

There is no power in the flesh of man to be one with another. The non-regenerated soul is self-seeking and gains nothing by cooperating with another to be one. The ease of oneness with others was destroyed with the act of disobedience in the garden. Jesus came to restore this oneness. The oneness between God and man and among brethren is one of the benefits of the cross. Therefore, oneness is possible, but not easy because of spiritual opposition.

To understand the spiritual opposition mankind faces, it is best to look at Ephesians 6:10. *For we wrestle not against flesh and blood, but against principalities, against powers, against spiritual wickedness in high places.* Paul describes the spiritual forces that are at work in the atmosphere against mankind and gives us insight into how to combat them. He list the weapons we are to use. The weapons listed are truth, righteousness, gospel of peace, faith, salvation, word of God, prayer, perseverance and supplication.

Note that all weapons are defensive except one, the sword of the spirit, which is the word of God. Paul was in prison when he wrote to the Ephesian church. He used the armor worn by Roman soldiers to give them a natural picture of the spiritual protection they have. Because an attack can come in various forms aimed at any part of the body, full body coverage was necessary to live after a blow from the enemy. Spiritually, Paul warned believers to protect their minds, hearts, reproductive ability, and their feet specifically.

> 2 Cor: 10:3-6 *"For though we walk in the flesh, we do not war after the flesh: (For the weapons of our warfare are not carnal, but mighty through God to the pulling down of strongholds;) Casting down imaginations, and*

Marriage: Work and Warfare

every high thing that exalteth itself against the knowledge of God, and bringning into captivity every thought to the obedience of Christ, And having readiness to revenge all disobedience, when your obedience is fulfilled."

To guard against the warfare that comes against the unity of oneness in marriage, spouses should insulate their marriage. How can a marriage be guarded against spiritual attacks? There are several things spouses can do in addition to previously mentioned recommendations to protect the oneness in their marriage. These include becoming one with Christ, praying, maintaining physical intimacy and renewing minds to the word of God.

The first step to becoming *one with Christ* is to accept that He is the Son of God who came to earth as man and died for our sins and victoriously arose from the dead. Once a person accepts Jesus Christ as savior, they have the choice of whether to grow spiritually or remain a carnal, immature believer. To grow up in Christ we must become one with His Word which is the Bible. Daily reading and applying the Bible will help us to become one with Christ. This is an important decision my husband and I both made before we met. We both had a relationship with God and were conforming into His image. Although we were spiritually mature, we expected each other to continue to grow. Today, we marvel at who we are and rejoice that we are not the people we married. We are better in our spirit, soul and body because of Jesus Christ.

Prayer is how we communicate with God. The most effect prayers are those that are based on scripture. God cannot refuse, reject or deny His Word. He esteems His Word above His name. Psalm 138:2. Spouses should not only pray individually, but also pray together and for each other.

Chapter 9 – The Warfare of Oneness

From the time of our first phone conversation, until now, my husband and I have maintained a daily time of morning and evening prayer together. Yes, we both pray individually to God, but we both agree that our time of praying together has been instrumental in putting out many of the fiery darts aimed at destroying our union. The prayer can be short or long, but most importantly, it gets us to agree on what is important to us and invites God to impart His wisdom, strength and blessings.

Maintaining sexual intimacy is so important, we are instructed to do this in Ephesians 7:3. The King James Version calls it "due benevolence." New International Version uses "marital duties." The Amplified Bible refers to it as "conjugal rights." In any translations, version or paraphrase all refer to married couples maintaining sexual intimacy. The reason this is important is explained in Ephesians 7:5 as not to cause one spouse to go outside of the marriage because of a lack of sexual self-control. Paul gives an exception to this during times of fasting when both spouse agree to abstain, but that intimacy should be renewed when fasting is completed. Noticed that he did not give illness as an excuse for withholding sexual intimacy.

The Corinthian church was flowing in the gifts of the Holy Spirit. He did not expect there to be illness among believers. One of the signs that a person is a believer is that they would lay hands on the sick and they would recover. If someone in the church was sick, believers should lay hands on them and they would not be sick anymore. My husband and I have proved this to be true. There was a time when I was not physically able to render his due benevolence because of pain in my body. He laid his hand on me, commanded the illness and pain to go. Guess what! It did! You can use the same power of God, name of Jesus and lay hands on your spouse or yourself and expect healing to manifest. Healing is a provision of the Kingdom of God.

Marriage: Work and Warfare

Jesus called it the children's bread in Matthew 15:22-28. If you are experiencing illness, sickness or disease put your hand in the area of your problem and read the following prayer a loud. Father, in the name of Jesus, I thank you that Jesus paid the price for my total healing according to Isaiah 53. By His stripes, I was healed. Therefore, any sickness, disease or illness in my body I command you to GO NOW! Pain, you are not permitted to afflict me anymore. PAIN, BE GONE, NOW in Jesus name. Whatever that is in my body that is preventing my healing from manifesting, Body you disintegrate, dissolve, get rid of NOW. Body, whatever is needed to manifest the healing I have, you generate now. Body, line up with the Word of God. Be Healed. Be Whole. Be full of life now. Now thank God for healing you. Go and enjoy life and your marriage.

Paul admonishes believers to be *renewed in their mind* in Romans 12:2. Before accepting Christ as Savior our minds have been continually fashioned after the world systems. We think and act according to the kingdoms of this world and not according to the kingdom of God. When our minds are renewed, we are able to live according to the Word of God and His Kingdom. To be renewed our minds must receive new information. This new information is found in the Word of God. We must study God's Word. Daily Bible study will help our spirit man to mature in Christ.

Although this chapter is about the warfare of oneness in marriage, it is filled with the importance of both spouses having a relationship with God through His Son, Jesus Christ. This is because the enemy that wants to destroy your marriage has been defeated by the savior of the soul. I do not believe our marriage would have survived the onslaught of attacks that have come against it if my husband and I were not strong believers in the Word of God and prayer. Whether you and your spouse are believers in Jesus or not you will need Him to navigate through married life. My prayer is that the truths in this book that have helped my marriage will lead you to the one who is truth and love, my savior, Jesus Christ.

Chapter 9 – The Warfare of Oneness

74

Marriage: Work and Warfare

Study Questions

1) We are three part beings: Spirit, Soul & Body.

    a. What is the purpose of each of these three?

2) "Life is basically, what you see is what you get. The physical is what I see and that is all that matters." These statements are false statements. Why are they false?

3) Study Ephesians Chapter 6:10 to understand the world we cannot see.

4) How can you guard your marriage against spiritual attacks?

5) Commit to renewing your mind daily by reading the word of God, meditating and acting on it.

Chapter 9 – The Warfare of Oneness

CHAPTER 10
THE CHARACTERISTICS OF A HEALTHY MARRIAGE

My husband and I have visited Israel several times. As we toured the country there were many buildings that were thousands of years old, still standing. Because of wars, fires, floods, earthquakes and other disasters throughout centuries, much has been destroyed, but there are stones that still stand. There are stones that have not been moved or broken. Foundations of stone that were laid centuries ago can still be built upon again. The most notable are the walls around Jerusalem and the stones used to build the temple. We stood over a portion of the wall that King Hezekiah built centuries ago that is still there.

Just as the stones of Jerusalem are standing, so can your marriage weather circumstances and tragedies that have and will come against it. What determines how your marriage manages the good and the not so good times is the foundation that is laid in the initial stages. How did your marriage begin? Is your marriage built upon truth, the word of God, love and respect for one another? If so, you have a strong foundation that can be built upon for years to come.

Beloved of God, it is possible to have not only a marriage that expands years, but also one of fulfillment, joy and peace. Just as no two people are the same, no two marriages are the same. Each spouse brings to the marriage experiences, knowledge and ideas that have molded them over the years into the individuals they have become. Do not expect your marriage to be the picture of the marriages you were exposed to in your youth. This is a different time of life. Many seasons have come and gone since then. Even the marriages you knew then are different now because of changes that have taken place in the individual spouses lives. Marriages that were held together at one season by the sacrifices made because of children or a business, is

Chapter 10 – The Characteristics of a Healthy Marriage

now glued by a responsibility to one another that cannot be destroyed by sickness and losses. Things that at one point seemed unforgiveable are now not just forgiven, but also forgotten. A love that was once burned with passion, is now what gives life meaning. Often in the winter season of life, spouses find joy in the comfort of the relationship that has grown throughout the years. Without it, they have no reason to endure life.

Your marriage is uniquely yours. It is not the marriage of your parents', friends' or any other people you admire or fear. Take the restrictive boundaries off your marriage that you may have placed because of your past. It is a new day. Free your spouse from limits that you may have placed on them because of what others may believe that he or she should be, do or become. Give your spouse the freedom to be who God created them to be. This is more of a problem early in marriage. Over time spouses learn that no matter how much you want the best for your mate, only God can change them. You cannot change your spouse. None of your words, threats, tears or even violence can bring about the permanent change that only the power of God can bring in your spouse.

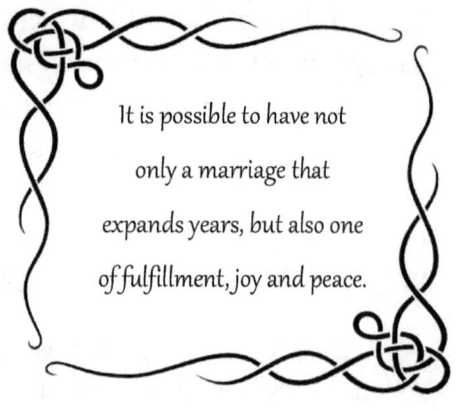

It is possible to have not only a marriage that expands years, but also one of fulfillment, joy and peace.

For your marriage to change, you must change. Change is not easy. It is uncomfortable and inconvenient. Nonetheless, it is for your good and the good of your marriage. Change is a process; it is not always instant. Be patient. Walk in love according to I Corinthians 13:4-8. You will not only see the fruit of your labor, but enjoy it. Do not give up. As you change, your spouse will change and so will your marriage change.

Marriage: Work and Warfare

Balance is important in every relationship, especially marriage. A spouse that focuses on the work of marriage and ignores the warfare of marriage will find themselves working in their own strength or efforts trying to make their marriage survive. A spouse who focuses on the warfare or spirituality of marriage will also find it difficult for their marriage to survive.

> *James 2:17, 20-22,24 "...Even so faith, if it hath not works, is dead, being alone. Faith without works is dead. Was not Abraham our father justified by works, when he had offered Isaac his son upon the altar? Seest thou how faith wrought with his works, and by works was faith made perfect? By faith a man is justified, and not by faith only but by works."*

Spouses should understand that both work and warfare are important in a healthy marriage.

Chapter 10 – The Characteristics of a Healthy Marriage

Marriage: Work and Warfare

Study Questions

1) Is your marriage healthy or on life support supplied by one spouse? Whether you have ever witnessed a healthy marriage or not, they do exist. Your marriage, too, can be healthy. Both spouses must be willing to do what is required for their marriage to be healthy.

2) Is your marriage in a season of transition? If so, be patient with your spouse. Pray through the season for the changes you desire to see in both of you.

CHAPTER 11
THE COMMUNICATION OF A HEALTHY MARRIAGE

"But speaking the truth in love, may grow up into him in all things, which is his head, even Christ: From whom the whole body fitly joined together and compacted by that which every joint supplieth, according to the effectual working in the measure of every part, maketh increase of the body unto the edifying of itself in love."

Ephesians 4:15

This scripture, in the context of the entire chapter and book, is referring to being mature in the doctrines of Christ and growing up in the fullness of him and not being deceived by false teachers distorting the truth and bring division within the body of Christ. Just as it is important to speak the truth in love within the church, it is also important in marriage. Remember, marriage is a picture of Christ's relationship with His bride, the church. Therefore, we can extract the principles in this verse and apply them to the marital relationship.

According to The Message Bible, 1 Corinthians 13:4-8 simply states that love never gives up. Love cares more for others than for self. Love doesn't want what it doesn't have. Love doesn't strut. Doesn't have a swelled head. Doesn't force itself on others. Isn't always "me first." Doesn't fly off the handle. Doesn't keep score of the sins of others. Doesn't revel when others grovel. Takes pleasure in the flowering of truth. Puts up with anything. Trusts God always. Always looks for the best. Never looks back. But keeps going to the end.

Each believer has been given grace in the measure of the gift of Christ. We should all come in to the unity in the Faith and the knowledge of the Son of God and mature spiritually. Each person in

Chapter 11 – The Communication of a Healthy Marriage

the body has a contributing role of support that fits together to complete the body. This is also true in marriage. Each spouse has a different, but equally important role of support in marriage to complete it. If unity and love is expected of believers, how much more should this unity and love be expressed in the marital relationship? Spouses must guard against outsiders infiltrating their marriage with deceitful, cunning words, which destroy the unity. Just like a puzzle that fits together to complete a picture, believers fit together to form the body of Christ. Spouses should fit together and their communication should be unified to resemble the unity in the body.

Study Questions

1) Memorize I Corinthians 13:4-8. Practice these daily, especially towards your spouse.

2) It is difficult to be in covenant with someone you are not willing to be truthful. Speak the truth in love.

3) Monitor your conversation with your spouse. How does your conversation measure with I Corinthians 13:4-8.

Chapter 11 – The Communication of a Healthy Marriage

Chapter 12
The Intimacy of a Healthy Marriage

In the Garden of Eden, man and woman lived together in fellowship with one another and with God. There were no clothing to cover their nakedness. Nor was there any shame in their created beings. Yes, they were different. Their being different was natural and accepted. *Genesis 2:25 "And they were both naked, the man and his wife, and were not ashamed."*

My husband and are opposites in many areas. One of them is intimacy. I had lived most of my life single and many years alone. My husband has a heart for marriage. Although he had been unsuccessful at it before, he still longed for an intimate spousal relationship. Therefore, he was more willing to reveal himself and not hide anything. It took more time for me to trust him. He was patient and loved me through this transition, which was not easy.

No matter how difficult your situation may be at this time, choose to walk in love. Allow your spouse the time and space he or she needs to adjust to this new relationship. If you are married and the vows were broken, be more sensitive to the time it may take for the offended spouse to forgive you and love again. It is possible. Trust must be reestablished. Love must be proved.

The intimacy of a healthy marriage is based upon transparency. Be transparent. When we are born we are born in our natural, created state. No clothing, only flesh. Clothing is only normal to us because we have become accustomed to it. If there are any remaining people groups who do not wear clothing of any type, I am unaware. This is because generally, when a village where nudity is normal is discovered, they are "normalized" with clothing.

Chapter 12 – The Intimacy of a Healthy Marriage

This need for outer covering is a sign of the inner covering over our hearts that we guard as we age. With age comes the knowledge of good, evil, pain and self-awareness. Trust becomes violated. Rejection is a reality. Offenses occur over and over again. All of these are the result of man's sin nature. Over the years, we layer our inner being with protection to guard us from harm. By the time we marry, there has been so many insults, it is difficult to trust our mates with who we really are.

As we allow God to heal our wounds. We can experience love, the kind of love that does not come to take, but to give...a love that wants what is best for us. Unconditional love can be trusted. As our spouses reveal more of themselves, we are free to reveal who we are. To allow our spouse to get to the core of our being takes time. Deposits must be made into our trust account before a withdrawal can be validated. This is what paves the road back to the garden atmosphere of being naked and not ashamed.

What is most important to you? Does your spouse know this about you? Is your spouse supportive of this area of your life? If not, why? What is it about yourself that you hold secret and that you cannot share with your spouse? What steps can you take toward being transparent with your spouse? What steps do you need your spouse to take for you to be comfortable being intimate from the heart?

Take time answer these questions individually. Share the answers with your spouse when you are ready to discuss them. This will help your spouse to know who you are or who you have become since marriage. It will also open the door for intimate conversation. It is helpful for both spouses to agree to give and receive constructive criticism that will help the other and the marriage improve.

Marriage: Work and Warfare

Study Questions

1) Healthy marriages are not perfect, but have learned to navigate the difficult times with finesses and love that covers their imperfections so flaws are not noticed. Is your marriage suffering from an attack that has threatened oneness? Do not give in or quit. You both can overcome.

2) Intimacy takes transparency. Are you comfortable revealing your self, spirit soul and body to your spouse? If not, why?

Chapter 12 – The Intimacy of a Healthy Marriage

CHAPTER 13
THE ONENESS OF A HEALTHY MARRIAGE

> *"Therefore, shall a man leave his father and his mother and shall cleave unto his wife: and they shall be one flesh."*
>
> *Genesis 2:24*

The phrase one flesh indicates covenant. A man is to leave his primary connection with his parents and began a unified connection with his wife. This new connection with his wife is now to become his primary human earthly relationship. He is to cleave or join to his wife. They are to be partners with one purpose. Be one with Christ. Be one in the spirit. Few marriages enter this level of oneness, even though its importance is explained in scripture. If the believer's marriage demonstrated this oneness, the world would see it and desire it. Therefore, they would desire the God who made it possible.

Healthy marriages enter oneness when they are in agreement in at least three areas: Language (Communication), Purpose (Actions) and Blood or Name (Covenant),

1. **LANGUAGE** - They speak the same language. Whether the question is asked to the husband or wife, the answer is the same. No one individual's desires are placed above the desires of the marriage. Jesus often explained that he only spoke what his father spoke. They are one and spouses, too should be one, speaking the same things.

2. **PURPOSE** - Jesus only did what he saw his father do. If you and your spouse have not come to an agreement on the purpose of your marriage, discuss it. You two should have the same expectations for your marriage. Spouses should walk in unity so that both know their limitations and what the other would do in a similar situation. At all

Chapter 13 – The Oneness of a Healthy Marriage

possible times, do what is best for the marriage at the cost of what is best for the individual.

3. **BLOOD OR NAME** - The father is in me and I am in the father. So, the husband should bear the wife and the wife bear the husband. This is not to cover up wrong doings, but to edify and be strength in place of the other's weaknesses. This is the purpose and power of covenant. I use my strengths to make strong my husband's weaknesses. He uses his strength to make strong my weaknesses. Therefore, when the world looks at us, they do not see our weaknesses, only strengths. My husband and I have the same name. We have access to the same wealth. If I destroy him, I ultimately destroy myself. If he harms me, he himself is harmed. We are one and cannot be divided. If I seek to shorten his life, my life will be affected because we are one.

Many times people look at us and assume I am the weak link to coming between us. They take my meekness for weakness and his boldness for strength. What they do not see is that we are intertwined so tightly that we are one. I know how he will respond and he knows how I would respond. We have the benefit of being each other in the others stead. I borrow his strength when needed and he uses mine. That is the power of oneness in a healthy marriage. This same benefit can become a hindrance if spouses do not walk in oneness.

Marriage: Work and Warfare

Study Questions

1) Is there agreement in your marriage in the areas of Communication, Actions and Covenant? If not what is lacking and why?

2) If you and your spouse have not done so, together decide what main purpose are you two uniting to achieve? Determine to speak the same language concerning it.

Chapter 13 – The Oneness of a Healthy Marriage

❧ Chapter 14 ❧
Conclusion

Marriages require work and warfare to maneuver through the storms of life. The areas of communication, intimacy and oneness are in need of the attention of both spouses to maintain a state of health. Marriage is God's fundamental building block for the family. Because of the high rate of divorce in western cultures, we see the fabric of our society degrading into a growing common belief that marriage is unnecessary. In the event that marriage is held in high esteem, governments are seeking to redefine marriage from God's original intent. Just because man changes what he considers legal does not mean that God will approve and endorse it. The Kingdom of God is not seeking the approval or permission of the governments of this world system. God's word is final. Marriage between man and woman is good.

It does not matter where you are in your marriage. Whether you are newly wedded or have been married most of your life. God's plan for your marriage goes beyond you not being alone. He wants others to look at your marriage and desire a relationship with Him. He wants to use your relationship with your spouse to demonstrate His love for the church. Whatever challenges you now face, evaluate them and determine if they are a result of the work you need to put into your marriage or the warfare you need to defeat.

The End

Go and Continue in Your Journey of Enjoying a Healthy Marriage

ADEGBAYI INTERNATIONAL MINISTRIES

Strengthening Marriages by Teaching

Kingdom Principles of Marriage

OUR MISSION is to encourage couples through Biblical principles and prayer to enjoy their marriage while fulfilling their God given purpose and to spread the Kingdom of God through sound Biblical teaching.

ADEGBAYI INTERNATIONAL MINISTRIES is committed to ministering to married and unmarried persons through these ministries:

- **AMBASSADORS TRAINING CENTER** is the weekly Bible Study in Duncanville, Texas where we teach the principles of Kingdom Living. Visit www.ambassadorstc.com for more information.

- **COVENANT RENEWAL CONFERENCE** empowers attendees to:
    - Embrace the power of forgiveness
    - Discover the favor of God in marriage
    - Understand the marriage covenant
    - Improve communication
    - Rekindle intimacy with spouse and God

  To schedule a Covenant Renewal Conference in your area, please submit a request at www.aim4love.org.

- **COVENANT LIVING RADIO** is the 24/7 audio broadcast and video is available on demand. For more information please visit www.covenantlivingradio.com.

- **COVENANT LIVING TOUR** coordinates group travel to Israel. We offer competitive rates for churches and ministries. For more information please visit www.covenantlivingtour.com.

- **COVENANT LIVING BREAKFAST** teaches men the purpose of man and the importance of woman. Many men have not been fathered or have not witnessed what a healthy marital relationship should be. This interactive and realistic workshop will be and unintimidating place for men to encourage each other. To schedule this event in your area, please submit request at www.aim4love.org.

- **AIM 4 LOVE DATE NIGHT** is an event held at local restaurants. The purpose is to help couples "date after marriage." Each event will have a theme that will focus on improving the marriage relationship. If you would like to have AIM4Love Date Night in your city, please submit a request at www.aim4love.org.

- **COVENANT LIVING FOR THE UNMARRIED** is designed to encourage the unmarried while preparing for marriage. Whether engaged or waiting for God to reveal their spouse to be, there are boundaries that should be set that will keep God first. This workshop can be 1-3 days. It is filled with truth and humor. There are men and women breakouts as well as questions and answer sessions. Certificates are given at the end of workshop. To schedule an event in your area, please submit request.

ADEGBAYI INTERNATIONAL MINISTRIES

P.O. Box 2549
Red Oak, TX 75154
972.217.1959
aim4love.org
www.aim4love1@gmail.com

www.ingramcontent.com/pod-product-compliance
Lightning Source LLC
LaVergne TN
LVHW021403080426
835508LV00020B/2441